PRAISE FOR

GROUPS OF 12

Great book! I read it through in one sitting. Joel Comiskey has extrapolated the basic biblical truths found in the G-12 model used in the International Charismatic Mission in Bogota, Columbia and makes them user-friendly for any pastor desiring to implement any of these values in the local church.

LARRY KREIDER
International Director, DOVE Christian Fellowship International

God has graciously poured out the new wine among us, and the G-12 model is the new wineskin that will contain the coming massive harvest.

JOHN ARNOTT
Sr. Pastor, Toronto Airport Christian Fellowship

This is a masterpiece! Joel Comiskey has made a significant contribution to the cell church movement with this book.

RALPH W. NEIGHBOUR, JR.
Founder, TOUCH Outreach Ministries, Inc.

Excellent! Comiskey gives the most comprehensive and insightful explanation of G-12 I have yet heard or read. Chapter seven alone is worth its weight in gold!

KAREN HURSTON
Hurston Ministries

Once I read this book, I knew exactly what to do next with our cell ministry. It answered key questions and pointed out dangerous pitfalls to avoid. Reading this book is more informative than going to Bogota and a lot cheaper. Comiskey's thorough research and first-hand experience combine to give us a powerful book that will help countless leaders.

JIM EGLI
Director of Training, TOUCH Outreach Ministries, Inc.

Understanding the foundational principles of ICM's G-12 model would help any church reach more souls, make strong disciples of Jesus Christ and have continuous growth. Joel Comiskey clearly articulates these principles and at the same time gives insights for flexible application in the North American church. This is a refreshing and eye-opening account of the G-12 cell church model.

BILLY HORNSBY
National Director, Bethany Cell Church Network

GROUPS OF 12

GROUPS OF 12

A NEW WAY TO MOBILIZE LEADERS AND MULTIPLY GROUPS IN YOUR CHURCH

JOEL COMISKEY

TOUCH PUBLICATIONS

Houston, Texas, U.S.A.

Published by TOUCH Publications
P.O. Box 19888
Houston, Texas, 77224-9888, U.S.A.
(281) 497-7901 • Fax (281) 497-0904

Cover design by Don Bleyl
Text design by Rick Chandler
Editing by Scott Boren

International Standard Book Number: 1-880828-15-4

TOUCH Publications is the book-publishing division
of TOUCH Outreach Ministries, a resource and consulting
ministry for churches with a vision for cell-based local
church structure.

Find us on the World Wide Web at
http://www.touchusa.org

CONTENTS

FOREWORD

When David Yonggi Cho was a young pastor, God gave him the vision of commissioning Korean believers to become leaders of cell groups. He pioneered the cell church patterns, hammering out details through many years of trial and error. A study of his church reveals an initial seven-year period when the cells doubled and doubled again. Then the ministry exploded like a rocket leaving the launch pad! At present, Pastor Cho not only pastors the largest church in the world but has also sent Korean missionaries into every corner of every continent.

This phenomenal growth came after much prayer and Spirit-given guidance. Prayer and fasting became the heartbeat of his equipping track as he inserted a zeal for harvesting into the hearts of every cell member. Those who have visited his ministry will observe the classic model of Cell, Congregation, and Celebration. It has taken 35 years to mature.

Many of us, including myself, have followed his pattern of structuring cell groups as the "Basic Christian Communities," church in its most basic form. This Korean pattern is called in this book the "Five by Five" (5x5) strategy.

In the past few years, an alternate structure for developing cells has been created by the Holy Spirit through the servant hearts of César and Claudia Castellanos in Bogota, Colombia. They have called this structure the "Groups of Twelve." It has been emerging year by year, led by the pastor and his "G-12." On my two visits to Bogota, it became evident that there were many fingerprints in the design of the structure. César Fajardo, one of the Twelve, has had a major part in its development. Others in the pastor's Group of Twelve have also contributed to the concepts and strategies now in use.

The development of Misión Carismática Internacional, reported in this book, is a report of moist, unhardened clay in the hands of Spirit-filled potters. It is now considered to be the second largest cell church in the world!

The "Principle of Twelve" has been adopted by churches everywhere. You will return to this book many times to reflect on the brilliant report made by Dr. Joel Comiskey. Pray God's richest blessings to be showered upon César and Claudia Castellanos, entrusted with this concept. Pray also about how you will apply the principles presented in this book to your own ministry.

Dr. Ralph W. Neighbour, Jr.

ACKNOWLEDGMENTS

Although my name stands alone on the cover of the book, I was not alone in writing it. The success of this book is because of the significant contributions of certain people. First and foremost, I want to thank my wife, Celyce, for her support, revisions, and encouragement. Second, I want to thank my editor, Scott Boren, who carefully guided the development of this book by taking a messy manuscript in its early stages and giving it order. Scott's expert guidance shaped this book in a significant way. Jim Egli provided foundational research on the G-12 model and freely shared it with me. I also want to thank the entire staff at the International Charismatic Mission and especially Luis Salas for helping me understand the G-12 model. Finally, I want to thank each pastor listed in chapters 10-11 for sending me summaries of how they adapted the G-12 model to their own context.

INTRODUCTION

The Groups of 12 movement (G-12) is spreading across the world like a wildfire. After implementing the G-12 model, the International Charismatic Mission in Bogota, Colombia (ICM), the founding church of this strategy, mushroomed from 70 small groups to 20,000 small groups in just eight years. Four of the largest cell churches in the world are now G-12 churches.[1] Reports come from India about churches there being transformed by this simple strategy. Since Bethany World Prayer Center, the most prominent cell church in the U.S., decided to adopt this model, many other North American churches have followed its lead. Churches want to understand the G-12 model, and more importantly, how to apply it to their unique situations.

One pastor traveled to ICM to "catch the fire" and learn about the G-12 model, and God transformed him during his time there. He witnessed healings, watched 18,000 people gather for a Saturday youth service, and grasped ICM's vision to reach a city. This pastor discovered how the 20,000 cells cared for the cell leaders and produced the amazing growth. He decided that his own church should follow the same route.

Like many before him, he went back to his church, desiring to implement this new strategy. Soon, however, he became discouraged. His congregation lacked the spiritual dynamics found at ICM. The church's prayer base was weak, and few people understood the need for small group multiplication. The six ingrown cells at his church resisted the thought of giving birth to new cells. His enthusiasm dwindled as he discovered that his circumstance differed from that of ICM.

Many return from Bogota pumped-up because of the revival atmosphere of ICM. They desire to copy the entire G-12 model but fall short by not discerning between transferable G-12 principles and those that are culturally bound.

Churches are also at a disadvantage when they try to implement the G-12 model because so little is published about it. Since so little is known about ICM, people travel to Bogota to understand the ICM system. This book can save you the trip.

Defining G-12

What is this G-12 model? Dr. Ralph Neighbour states, "The G-12 model is confusingly simple."[2] Is it a new focus on discipleship? Another cell system? An emphasis on homogeneous groups? The following chapters will define the G-12 model and remove the shroud of mystery that hangs over it. But before delving into the inner workings of the G-12 system, some initial observations are necessary.

First, the G-12 model does not effectively replace the cell church system. Rather, it can improve your cell church system by increasing your capability to develop leaders and multiply groups. It can fine-tune your cell church system, but it will not replace the cells. César Castellanos, the founder of ICM declares:

> The International Charismatic Mission has grown so rapidly and has impacted the world because of our cell structure. I have arrived at the conclusion, after becoming acquainted with other ministries in different countries, that the best method for a church to grow is through home cell groups. We left behind all of our programs that absorbed so much of our time (and produced few results), and we established only one program: cell ministry.[3]

The G-12 model (or a combination thereof) provides a way to fine-tune your cell church for growth. It requires less structure and flows nicely from the grass roots level. It won't, however, make you a cell church.

Second, the G-12 model preserves the fruit of evangelism. Castellanos says, "The G-12 model is not for your church to grow. What gives the growth is the evangelistic work. The G-12 model is God's strategy to conserve the fruit."[4] The key, according to César, is evangelism. Many people want to learn the G-12 model, but they're not winning the multitude. The advice of César Castellanos is to first win the multitude and then preserve the fruit through the G-12 model.[5]

Third, the crowning principle of the G-12 model is that it views every member as a potential cell leader. All cell leaders at ICM seek to transform their cell members into cell leaders. The G-12 model is essentially a leadership multiplication strategy.

Fourth, the G-12 model will fine-tune and improve your pastoral care for cell leaders. For years, the cell church primarily used the Jethro model (5x5 structure) to care for cell leadership. The G-12 model has given the cell church a new alternative, a new way to look at cell church ministry.

The G-12 model holds every cell leader accountable to a higher authority while taking responsibility for younger, emerging cell leaders. César Castellanos said, "This model totally eliminates the problem of care because everyone is cared for by a leader of 12."[6]

LOOKING BENEATH THE OBVIOUS

I visited ICM in 1996, 1997, 1998, and 1999. Each visit was nearly a year apart, so I was able to discern significant progression in the G-12 model and analyze it over time. My original research was part of my Ph.D. degree at Fuller Theological Seminary. I have analyzed its material (mostly in Spanish), attended its meetings, and interviewed its leaders.[7]

Because ICM is constantly changing as it follows the Spirit of God, I had to dig below the surface structure in order to delineate vital G-12 principles. After you understand these principles, you should apply them to your own situation.

This book is far more than a theoretical exercise. I serve as one of the pastors in a cell church called the Republic Church in Quito, Ecuador. My senior pastor, Porfirio Ludeña, visited ICM on two different occasions. He patiently guided our cell church in the transition to the G-12 model. We, as a pastoral team, wrestled with applying G-12 principles in our context. More importantly, we had to determine which principles we wanted to apply in our church. At this point, we have fully transitioned to the G-12 model. But our G-12 strategy is different from the Bogota model. I predict that your transition will also result in a unique model. God desires each cell church to use its creativity.

While this book will explain the original G-12 model of the International Charismatic Mission, it does not endorse all aspects of that model. You don't have to be "charismatic" nor in agreement with ICM to benefit from the G-12 principles. Instead, a clear understanding of ICM should guide you to the crucial principles that you can apply in your church.

IS THE G-12 FOR YOU?

If you desire to view each person as a potential leader or want to know how to integrate each person into your training system, the G-12 model will provide the missing link. Churches throughout the world are discovering that G-12 principles provide effective discipleship and pastoral care for new cell leaders. You don't have to apply the entire structure of ICM to benefit from the G-12 principles.

If you're just not quite sure about the G-12 model, by the time you finish this book you will understand the fundamental G-12 principles and should know which ones apply to your particular situation.

BUILDING

ON A VISION

Some problems are wonderful — like church growth so rapid you must rent a football stadium to contain it. What about renting the stadium and then immediately needing two services? Can you imagine a Saturday night youth service drawing 18,000 people each week?

Welcome to the International Charismatic Mission where prayer and a revival atmosphere are a way of life. Begun with eight people meeting in a living room, it has captured the world's attention because of the powerful work of God's Holy Spirit.

ICM is giving the world a new perspective on Colombia, a country better known for drug peddling and guerrilla warfare than rapid church growth. About Colombia, the world's chief exporter of cocaine, Patrick Johnstone writes, "Corruption, blackmail, kidnapping, assassination and revenge murders have brutalized society."[1]

Yet where sin abounds, God manifests His amazing grace. Pastor Castellanos stood against the tide of sin and grasped a different future for his country. People are now hearing about Colombia in a positive light. They can't talk enough about God's amazing work through the G-12 groups. Christ is conquering the darkness of sin and Satan and showing the rest of the world how dynamic growth happens.

TESTIMONY OF CÉSAR CASTELLANOS

César Castellanos was the eighth child in a family of 12. Due to his father's untimely death, his mother raised the entire family.[2] César, like many teenagers, experimented with drugs and sought answers apart from Jesus Christ.

As a university student in 1972, he became annoyed with his philosophy professor, who continually attacked the Christian faith. With the Bible in one hand, this professor dared anyone to prove him wrong. César accepted the challenge, although not a believer at the time. God in His sovereignty used an atheistic professor to stir him to study the Bible.[3]

As César began to read Genesis, God revealed Himself. God's presence flooded the room with a brilliant light, and César submitted himself to Jesus Christ. Christ transformed César freeing him from drugs and alcohol. The Holy Spirit filled the void, granting him a hunger for God's Word.[4]

DISAPPOINTMENT IN MINISTRY

Filled with a burning passion for Jesus Christ, Castellanos began proclaiming the gospel message on the streets of Colombia. Like John Wesley and George Whitefield, he carried his message to the masses. Castellanos also preached from pulpits and for nine years pastored several small churches among a variety of denominations. No extraordinary success marked those early years of ministry. Like Moses,

God was preparing Castellanos on the backside of the desert.

He grew frustrated by the lack of commitment and discipleship among his new converts. People received Christ, entered the church and quickly escaped through the back door. The traditional methods of church growth brought little lasting fruit.

God brought him to a breaking point.[5] Under the urging of the Holy Spirit, he resigned from the pastorate to wait on God and determine His will. "Lord, I'm not going to commit myself to anyone until you speak to me. I need to know what You want me to do," he said.[6] And God spoke.

GOD SPEAKS

"What kind of church would you like to pastor?" God asked Castellanos in 1983. He pictured a church of 120, the size of his largest church. Castellanos explains:

> I was striving to expand that number in my mind, but I couldn't. So I began to look at the sand of the seashore. As I looked at it, each grain of sand became a person, and I began to see hundreds of thousands of people. Then the Lord said: "That and much more I will give you, if you are in my perfect will."[7]

Encouraged by the vision, Castellanos started another church, this time in his living room. He named his church the "International *Charismatic* Mission" as an evangelistic strategy to reach Catholics. In the 1980s, the Colombian Catholic majority (97%) rejected the name "Evangelical" but was more open to the term "Charismatic."

This time Pastor César began with God's anointing, vision and commitment to making clear goals. His first goal was to reach 200 people in six months. He writes, "I could see the people arriving. There were so many I could see them forming lines. People were waiting for others to leave so they could get in. From that moment on, everything I have done and everything I do is based on faith!"[8] In just three months, there were 200 people!

FOLLOWING THE KOREAN MODEL

Pastor César's trip to Korea in 1986 provided foundational principles for establishing a cell church system. He and his wife Claudia returned transformed by the potential for unlimited church growth. Castellanos always believed in the role of small groups, but in 1986, he grasped the need for a cell church system as the way to support the growth of small groups.

Having only one model to follow, ICM copied Dr. David Yonggi Cho's system in its entirety. Pastor César organized his small groups geographically throughout Bogota. As he reflected back, he acknowledged that the early system needed fine-tuning. While copying the entire model, he failed to adapt it to his own cultural context. ICM limped along from 1986 to 1991, hoping for success but sensing that something was missing. The cells grew, but very slowly. By the end of 1991, there were only 70 cell groups.

THE REVELATION OF THE 12

Castellanos cried out, "Lord, I need something that will help me accelerate the growth."[9] God showed him the missing link, revealing the concepts that have become known as the G-12 model. This revelation, according to Castellanos, was like Newton discovering the law of gravity. César imagined Newton watching apples fall to the ground until, one day, he began asking himself some questions like, "Why does the apple fall directly to the ground? Why doesn't it fall upwards? Or to the side?"

Castellanos' discovery began similarly as he read about Jesus and his 12 disciples. Although he had read this passage many times previously, this time he saw something new. "Why 12 disciples? Why not 13? Why didn't he train the multitudes?" As he began to ask himself these questions, like an apple falling from a tree, God led him to the concept of the 12.[10]

The passage was Matthew 9:35-10:1:

Jesus went through all the towns and villages, teaching in their synagogues, preaching the good news of the kingdom and healing every disease and sickness. When he saw the crowds, he had compassion on them, because they were harassed and helpless, like sheep without a shepherd. Then he said to his disciples, "The harvest is plentiful but the workers are few. Ask the Lord of the harvest, therefore, to send out workers into his harvest field." He called his 12 disciples to him and gave them authority to drive out evil spirits and to heal every disease and sickness.

Jesus called his 12 disciples, knowing that the harvest was too plentiful for one person to reap it. He needed to work through others to minister to the masses. Christ chose 12 disciples to help Him carry out His Father's work. The 12 were His helpers, his assistants in the work.

Jesus stayed with his 12 disciples continually. They were His "long-term" or "permanent" disciples. He laughed with them, rejoiced with them, and taught them daily lessons. He would say to them, "Observe this." Afterwards, he would ask, "What did you discover?" On one occasion, Christ's disciples observed the generous offerings of the religious leaders compared to the two copper coins of the poor widow. Jesus taught them that the widow offered more because she gave from her poverty (Luke 21:1-4). Jesus took advantage of each situation to teach his disciples. He went everywhere with them in order to prepare them and train them for the harvest. Castellanos writes:

> I began to see Jesus' ministry with clarity. The multitudes followed, but He didn't train the multitudes. He only trained 12, and everything he did with the multitudes was to teach the 12. Then the Lord asked me another question: "If Jesus trained 12, should you win more than 12 or less than 12?"[18]

Castellanos sensed the revelation was from God. He was dissatisfied with his cell system that had produced only 70 cell groups. With this new knowledge, he began to pour his life into his leaders, just like Jesus. Castellanos expected his own 12 to do likewise — to find their own 12 and to reproduce Christ's likeness in them.

WAITING ON GOD'S TIMING

"Lord, I want to start immediately," Castellanos thought. But God said, "Wait." The Lord showed him that his co-pastor wanted to divide the church. He wanted to establish his own kingdom. God said, "If this man understands the vision that I'm giving to you and begins to multiply this vision, in one year, he'll develop disciples and later divide the church with them." This was a painful time for Castellanos, much like what Jesus suffered at the hands of Judas.[12]

Although God had shown Pastor César that this man wanted to divide the church, there was no concrete evidence, so Castellanos had to wait. Eventually this co-pastor began to manifest a spirit of rebellion and personal ambition, but by that time his authority was reduced to pastoring a satellite church in a distant city. When he finally tried to divide the church, he only attracted five families and eventually left ICM altogether.[13]

HARVEST TIME

When the time was right, Castellanos chose 12 disciples, with whom he met every week. His disciples followed the same pattern with their disciples. César Fajardo, the brother-in-law of César Castellanos and one of Castellanos' original 12, began to disciple 12 leaders among the young people. The G-12 system worked so well with the youth that it quickly spread throughout the church.[14] As they worked and developed the system of the 12, God began to give ICM unprecedented growth.[15]

From 1991 to 1994, the cells grew from 70 to 1200. But the real home cell explosion took place from 1995-1999. During 1996 alone the cells grew from 4,000 to 10,500. By 1999 there were 20,000 cell groups and some 45,000 people attending the celebrations in the indoor stadium and ten satellite churches throughout Bogota.[16] César says: "We've grown so much that we don't even count people anymore — just cell groups."[17]

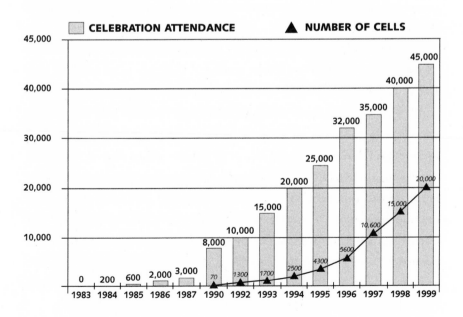

ATTACK ON CÉSAR CASTELLANOS

On Sunday in May 1997, a motorcycle pulled ahead of Pastor César and his family as they stopped at a red light. The rider drew a machine gun and opened fire on their car. Pastor César took five shots and his wife, Claudia, was shot once. The children were unhurt.

This vicious attack shocked the Evangelical world, yet the fervent prayers that followed this ghastly attack resulted in the glory of God. God healed Pastor César and Claudia, and there isn't any noticeable sign that César was ever wounded. Pastor César's survival is a miracle; the doctors were amazed that the bullet passed through his neck without hitting his voice box or spine, while another shot would have pierced his heart had his watch not deflected it away.

This was not the first attack on Castellanos. Two weeks before the shooting, burglars broke into his house and tied up his family as well as two visiting ministers before making off with all their electronic equipment. Colombia is certainly living up to its reputation as the most violent nation on earth.[18]

After the assassination attempt, Castellanos confessed, "I was afraid all the time. I couldn't pray like I used to." God began to speak to him and one day said, "I want you to forgive those men who tried to kill you." This was extremely difficult for Pastor César to hear because he had actually prayed that their gray hairs would go down to hell. But he sought God's help. He began to pray for the killers and even blessed those who attempted to end his life. When he finished praying, a weight fell from his shoulders. God's joy filled his soul. God once again lifted him up from the ash heap and began to transform his ministry. He learned an important lesson: "Never allow circumstances to kill your dreams."[19]

Those who are greatly used by God often pass through deep valleys. God knows what He's doing, although often we don't understand.

When God wants to drill a man, and thrill a man, and skill
    a man
When God wants to mold a man to play the noblest part;
When he yearns with all his heart to create so great and bold
    a man
That all the world shall be amazed; Watch His methods, watch
    His ways!
How He ruthlessly perfects whom He royally elects!
How he hammers him and hurts him, and with mighty blows
    converts him
Into trial shapes of clay which only God understands;
While his tortured heart is crying, and he lifts beseeching
    hands
How he bends but never breaks, when his good
    He undertakes
How He uses whom He chooses and with every purpose fuses
    him
By every act induces him, to try His splendor out —
God knows what He's about![20]

MORE DREAMERS NEEDED

God first gave Joseph a dream (Gen. 37). Later He prepared Joseph to fulfill that dream. If Joseph had not been Egypt's prisoner, he would never have become Egypt's governor. God gives dreams and visions but only fulfills them through prepared vessels — those who have been Egypt's prisoner.

César Castellanos started like the rest of us. He labored, experimented, and failed. He arrived at the end of his own resources, but then God revealed Himself in a new way. God uncovered the way to fine-tune his cell church philosophy.

God is preparing you for a special purpose. He wants to fulfill his dream in you. "Watch His methods; watch His ways."

2

BEHIND

THE NUMBERS

In 1972, NASA launched the exploratory space probe Pioneer 10. The satellite's primary mission was to reach Jupiter, photograph it and its moons and beam data to earth about the planet's magnetic field, radiation belts, and atmosphere. Scientists regarded this as a bold plan because up until then no satellite had gone beyond Mars. Pioneer 10 far exceeded the expectations of its designers, not only zooming past Mars, but also Jupiter, Uranus, Neptune and Pluto. By 1997, twenty-five years after its launch, Pioneer 10 was more than six billion miles from the sun. And despite the immense distance, the satellite continues to beam back radio signals to scientists on Earth. How does Pioneer 10 continue to send signals? An eight-watt transmitter. The key to the continual success of Pioneer 10 is the power source.

Some examine ICM and say that the G-12 system is the secret to its success. But there is much more to this church than structure. The 18,000 young people on Saturday night, the exciting worship and the

G-12 structure only form the outer shell — a shell that is empty without the power source.[1] To understand ICM's success, you must examine the church's power source and values.

You must not study the G-12 model in a vacuum. It's only part of a greater whole. There are other factors working in the background at ICM that have primed this church to grow so rapidly. Study these characteristics while you check the spiritual health of your own church.

MORE THAN METHODS

ICM does not forget what most people fail to acknowledge — the success of the church is primarily due to the blessing of God rather than the structural changes. This lesson is often lost to North American Christians. Without explicitly saying it, many assume that the G-12 structure will produce the fruit.

Pastor César gives the example of one pastor who changed his church's name to International Charismatic Mission, hoping to somehow capture the anointing of the church. Another pastor changed the chairs at his church to be just like ICM. Yet, the church failed to grow.[2]

During my third and fourth visit to ICM, I finally stopped focusing on the method and began to explore the spiritual characteristics of the church. Since the G-12 structure was already familiar to me by that time, I felt the liberty to examine ICM's commitment to fasting and prayer, the high priority of vision and goals and the key role that César Castellanos has played throughout the years. Scientifically, it's impossible to say that ICM is growing because of the G-12 structure. There are too many other dynamics at work.

If prayer is not important in your church, for example, can you expect the same results? If your church doesn't value submission to authority, can you expect all leaders to disciple 12 who will disciple 12 more? Cell ministry, along with a dynamic leadership care structure will enhance a church, but other dynamics must also be present in order for rapid growth to happen. Those desiring to apply this model must first possess a great respect for the work of God's Spirit and be ready to follow Him rather than mere structure.

ICM doesn't hold tightly to methods, since it is following the leading of the Spirit of God and creating its structures as they move ahead. Listen to Castellanos:

> Some pastors have the mentality of a century ago. They want to do the work like Finny or Spurgeon. But I want you to know that the actor on life's stage today is you. God has a new fresh anointing for you. He wants to release this anointing for you. Sacrifice that method.[3]

ICM is a moving target rather than a fixed one. The church is willing to change in order to fine-tune and develop its cell church experiment. Each time I've visited ICM, I've noticed major changes.[4] Frank Gonzalez, one of Castellanos' 12 disciples, says, "The secret behind our growth is not the cell groups nor the G-12 model — nor any other method. God doesn't anoint methods. The secret of our success is the manifestation of God's Spirit in our church."[5]

CORE VALUES

Every church prioritizes certain spiritual truths over others. ICM is no exception. They practice what they value. The following values come from the priorities of ICM. These values proceed from the top leadership and are practiced by all.

Passionate Spirituality

Spirituality is a way of life at ICM. It's a core value that you can see and feel. Castellanos and his entire leadership team live in the realm of spiritual warfare and divine guidance. But spirituality is a broad term. The dictionary simply defines it as the "state, quality, manner, or fact of being spiritual."[6] What exactly does "spirituality" mean? At ICM spirituality is seen in at least three areas:

1. Prayer. Prayer taps into God's resources. At ICM, someone is praying around the clock. ICM recognizes that only powerful prayer will break the hold of Satan over Colombia. Through prayer, ICM believes that it will triumph over the evil spirits controlling the drug trade, the guerrilla warfare, and government corruption.

Every morning from 5 A.M. to 9 A.M., people are praying in the church. A different pastor or leader is in charge of each hourly segment. Between 500-1000 people are present in the four morning sessions. Each Friday night, the church holds an all-night prayer meeting. On special occasions (as conditions in the country worsen due to drug trafficking and guerrilla warfare), the church dedicates one 24-hour, non-stop period to pray for the country.[7] Castellanos says: "Satan has deceived many pastors by making them so busy that they don't have time for prayer."[8]

Colombian Christians treat spiritual warfare very seriously. Identifying evil spirits and praying against the powers of darkness is continually practiced. At one point, the young people targeted in prayer a red-light disco district on a hillside near the church. The young people prayed against the demons of promiscuity and asked God for a sign of a spiritual breakthrough. The following day the main disco on the hillside burned to the ground!

César Castellanos believes that winning people for Christ involves walking in the miraculous on a continual basis. He says, "To win souls, you have to enter spiritual warfare."[9] Freddy Rodriguez says, "You can't evangelize unless you've entered into spiritual warfare. There are spiritual beings that govern the world. You have to take authority over these spirits."[10]

2. Fasting. Fasting and prayer complete the one-two punch at ICM. Pastor Castellanos requires that all his leadership engage in prayer and fasting.[11] In the early days, the church fasted for three days continually. God cleansed the airwaves and gave them revival. In October 1997, the men's network prayed and fasted for 85 days.[12] The whole church does this at least once per year. People visiting the church can literally feel the Spirit of God and the sense of revival.

3. Holiness. Holiness is another key to ICM's success. Many ministries have fallen into spiritual pride. Success is harder to handle than failure, and truly, ICM is highly successful. It would be easy to hold lavish conferences in order to boast about the G-12 model. Yet, ICM constantly promotes holiness; nothing less will do.

Every weekend there are numerous three-day retreats for the purpose of promoting holiness. ICM isn't satisfied with "decisions" that result in superficial Christian living. The call to holiness has stirred them to deal with the demonic bondage plaguing new believers. ICM realizes that its success is intimately tied to living purely and righteously before God.

Those at ICM have learned to pay the price for their Christian authority, even though it is costly. The young people do not attend cinemas, or go to discos. One ICMer who served as the English interpreter for a group became quite upset when the group continued looking at wall plaques that carried images of Inca gods. Those at ICM don't play with sin. They deal with it.

Authority and Submission
Pastor Castellanos, who is considered an apostle, is the founder and unchallenged leader. Those under Pastor Castellanos willingly obey

and follow him. Those same disciples under Pastor Castellanos also expect submission and obedience from their disciples. This value of submission runs down the ladder all the way to the new believer. Submission to authority makes the G-12 model run smoothly.

On various occasions, for example, I've asked for the most recent cell statistics from those in high positions at ICM. "Sorry, I don't have authorization to give you those statistics. I'll have to ask César Castellanos." At first I was offended. "Why make such a big deal about a simple request?" I wondered. Yet, upon further reflection I've come to realize that submission to higher-level authority is a common thread that runs through the entire system.[13]

This is an important value to remember when you think about transitioning to the G-12 model. Submission is one value that is not easy to copy, yet it makes the G-12 model workable. I submit to the leader over me, and I expect submission from those under me.

Time Commitment

One of the ICM training manuals declares, "Often, while others are sleeping, the leader continues working, trying to find solutions for the problems of the group."[14] One of the secrets of ICM's success is the high time commitment of the leadership. ICMers are sold out to the Lord's work, and their time commitment reflects that fact. The G-12 model, as practiced at ICM, is time-intensive.

Most cell leaders attend at least three cell-related meetings per week as well as the weekly congregational and celebration meetings. Cell leaders often have five cell-related meetings per week. In fact, I attended one meeting in which cell leaders were exhorted to direct three groups.[15] The time commitment of the following youth leader illustrates how the people of ICM feel about their call to ministry:

I met an 18-year-old student with 380 youth cells under her. Each week she attends a Group of 12 leadership cell in addition to leading her own leadership and evangelistic cells. She practices three days a week as a youth worship team dancer. She ministers in the Saturday evening youth service and teaches in the School of Leaders on Sunday morning.[16]

The phrase "a beehive of activity" best describes the constant action at ICM. "Church" never stops, from the early morning prayer meetings at 5 A.M. to services in the evening. When I first visited ICM in 1996, I stayed in the apartment within the main sanctuary (a converted sound room). I awoke at 5 A.M. every morning to worship music. I went to bed with praise and preaching every evening. Someone was busy in the church all day. There was rarely a moment when one of the pastors or lay people was not preaching the Word of God, worshipping or praying.[17]

Tight-knit Church Culture
At ICM you either fully accept the vision or you don't; you're either an insider or an outsider. The "inner workings" of the G-12 philosophy are reserved for those who are committed to it.

I discovered that ICM was very much like the successful companies that C. Collins & Jerry I. Porras analyzed in their excellent book *Built to Last: Successful Habits of Visionary Companies*. Collins and Porras studied highly successful companies over the long haul and then compared them with counterpart companies that didn't quite measure-up.

Among other characteristics, the authors discovered that promotion in the successful companies was reserved for those who "fit-in" and totally accepted the company culture. The successful, visionary companies were totally committed to their philosophy. The authors say,

. . . the visionary companies have such clarity about who they are, what they're all about, and what they're trying to achieve, they tend to not have much room for people unwilling or unsuited to their demanding standards. The visionary companies were more demanding of their employees and expected them to fit in with the company line.[18]

In the successful companies, employees spend large amounts of time with other employees from the same company and begin to buy into a company culture. The authors write, "New hires . . . immediately find nearly all of their time occupied by working or socializing with other members of 'the family,' from whom they further learn about the values and practices."[19]

ICM fits the description of these successful companies. Those who rise to higher positions of leadership believe so strongly in the church's philosophy that they are willing to commit huge amounts of time to further the church's vision. They demonstrate a complete submissiveness to authority and seek to avoid all criticism and negativity. The "tight-knit" culture of ICMers and their dedication to pursue shared values, help explain the success at ICM.

Miracles and the Power of God

ICM lives in the world of miracles and the supernatural. "Do you want crowds to flock to your church?" Pastor Castellanos asks. "Do the miracles of Jesus."[20] Castellanos believes that the G-12 model " . . . has a tremendous anointing for miracles."[21] Christ demonstrated his power and healing because of His compassion for the multitude. Castellanos says, "The model of the 12 was birthed in the compassion of Jesus when he saw the disorientation of the people."[22]

ICM consistently holds miracle services. Pastor Castellanos tells of a miracle service where ten paralytics sat in wheelchairs on the front row. He felt a tremendous compassion for them. He got down from the platform to pray for them thinking, "Lord, if nothing happens, at least I've tried." He asked each one of them to share their needs. As the third one began to explain his sickness, César felt that he had the faith to be healed. While César was praying (with his eyes still closed), this man was in front of the crowd standing up! César said, "Bring your chair in front. This chair has pushed you for a long time, and now you shall push it!"[23]

Vision

Castellano's congregation knows that he spends large amounts of time in prayer and communion with the Holy Spirit. In those times, he receives the worldwide vision for his church. Like the apostles of old, Castellanos has been very successful in passing down his vision to his top leadership. Several of his key leaders attribute their own success to the vision and inspiration of their pastor.

Pastor Castellanos has passed on the importance of visions and dreams to his disciple, César Fajardo. Pastor Fajardo teaches, "The vision must take hold of your life, and you must be able to transmit that vision. Sometimes the vision that you have will seem strange to others."[24]

Fajardo has learned this truth from experience. When he started the youth ministry at ICM in 1987, there were only 30 young people present. He began to dream of reaching the lost youth of Bogota. When he preached, he imagined that the place was filled. He openly declared to his small group, "There will come a time when young people will have to line-up to enter this church." In 1987, Fajardo took a photograph of the nearby indoor stadium full of people. He then hung that photograph on the wall in his room and began to dream and believe God to fill it with young people.[25]

Today, 18,000 young people line-up to gather on Saturday nights in that same indoor stadium. About 8,000 youth cell groups provide care for these masses. Approximately 500 youth receive Christ during each Saturday night service. The youth vision is contagious. These visiting pastors caught it:

> The atmosphere was electric with the Holy Spirit — to watch these young people worship with such fervor and pray with such intensity was a deeply moving experience, and I found myself weeping throughout the service. This meeting is a giant reaping machine as we discovered in all of their services. The preaching was hot and straight — Youth Pastor César Fajardo spoke on tearing down the lies of the devil. At the end of his ministry four to six hundred young people responded for salvation. The converts were then escorted (led by a man carrying a flag) to another hall through streets lined with people waiting for the next meeting who applauded them. Once in that hall they were preached to, registered and followed-up.[26]

Pastor Fajardo passes on his vision to his 12 disciples; those disciples have 12 more and the process continues down to the new young people who enter each week. Vision runs deep at ICM. It's contagious. Spiritual superstars develop easily in this atmosphere, but the vision begins at the top.

Goal-Setting

Those at ICM take their goals seriously. Pastor Castellanos asks each of the cell leaders to make goals for cell multiplication. Every three months the leaders at ICM review their goals, and at that time the leaders confirm both the short-term and long-term goals.[27] Every cell must multiply at least once per year, but cell leaders are encouraged to multiply their cell groups every six months.[28] Each cell must evangelize, win others, and eventually multiply.

César Castellanos says, "Our future projection must come through definite goal-setting. All of the growth that we've obtained thus far has come by focusing on specific goals."[29] He goes on to say: "Since the beginning of ICM, the Lord revealed to me the importance of defining goals and since that time, I've always focused on goals.[30] He says,

> Goals place rails on our faith; they arm us with a clear path — not to help God, but to help us! Clear goals help us to evaluate our work because all of our work must bear fruit. The church must make specific goals, which will help in the growth of the church. Understanding this, we must abandon traditional customs of many services without any purpose and remember to have one celebration and many cell groups throughout the week. In our case, after the church was growing rapidly we started other specialized services, but only those that helped us reach the main goal.[31]

Church Growth

Even before implementing the G-12 model, the International Charismatic Mission was committed to reaching Bogota with the gospel of Jesus Christ. Church growth is highly valued and esteemed at ICM. Pastor Castellanos says, "Some people talk about wanting only quality and not quantity. But God is concerned about both — quality and quantity. The church that doesn't grow is like stagnated water. The church that doesn't grow begins to turn in on itself and sows all kinds of wickedness."[32] He goes on to say,

> A church must not start in January with a certain number and have the same number by the end of December . . . this is a

reflection that the church is not fulfilling the great commission. This type of fruitlessness normally occurs in churches that are loaded down with programs that absorb their energy but don't produce evangelistic results . . .[33]

Because ICM evangelizes at every opportunity, there is a constant flow of new people. The goal of winning new people for Jesus Christ never stops. Sunday morning services, for example, are seeker-sensitive. Castellanos does everything possible to make them palatable to non-Christians. Every Sunday, hundreds receive Jesus Christ and are quickly integrated into the cell system. The first priority for ICM is to win people to Jesus Christ.

The larger ministries (men, women, spiritual warfare, young people, etc.) gather in congregational settings on weekdays for the purpose of edification *and* evangelism. There is always an invitation to receive Christ, and the new believers are immediately connected to a cell group from within that particular ministry.

The primary church growth method at ICM is evangelization through the multiplication of cell groups. All cells at ICM are evangelistic, and ICM believes that the "lion share" of successful evangelism takes place in the cell groups.

Creativity

ICM believes in adapting its methodology to more effectively reap the harvest. They're pragmatic. They're willing to test and experiment for the purpose of saving and discipling more souls for Christ's glory. Because the old cell system wasn't producing the desired results, they created the G-12 system.

Even after developing the G-12 strategy, ICM continues to adapt its methods. This attitude resembles the life and ministry of John Wesley. Richard Wilke writes:

John Wesley changed his structures and methods, almost against his will, in order to save souls. He didn't want to use women, but he did in exceptional circumstances. The 'exceptional' became normal. He didn't want to use lay pastors, but he did. They were able to reach the unbelievers. He didn't want to preach in the open air, but he did so that more might hear the Word of God.[34]

God desires to give you this same type of creativity for the sake of the harvest.

The Importance of the Couple

ICM believes strongly in the ministry of couples. Castellanos says,

Some pastors do not involve their wives in the ministry. They think that the place of the wife is only to care for children. I want to say to you that if your wife is not involved in the ministry, you will always have a lame ministry. God calls a man and a wife. God's calling is on the couple. Husbands must involve their wives in the ministry.[35]

Claudia Castellanos stands at the side of her husband, praying as well as speaking.[36] Claudia has modeled visionary leadership and even formed part of the Colombian senate in 1989 and has considered running for the presidency of Colombia. Almost half of the ICM staff is female.[37] If a married man feels called to ministry at ICM, he must be ready to minister with his wife.

This is a refreshing and powerful change in Latin American ministry, which has long been dominated by the "macho" man or the "caudillo" pastor. Only God knows how much this factor has affected the growth at ICM, but it's a very positive development in Latin American ministry.

CELL CHURCH VISION

When studying the G-12 model at ICM, it's important to remember the prior commitment to cell church ministry. After the cell church philosophy was firmly rooted in the church, ICM adjusted its cell church strategy for a greater harvest.

During the initial years of the church, small groups were important, but they weren't the heart of the church. You could say that at that time, ICM was a "church with cells." Then ICM reorganized totally around cell groups in 1986.

After implementing the G-12 strategy in 1991, ICM remains a cell church. The people at ICM understand the cell church philosophy and openly promote it. César says, "The success of church growth belongs to the cell church model. I don't know of any more powerful model than this."[38] Claudia Castellanos said, "Those churches that fail to develop cell churches will be left behind."[39] Claudia describes the traditional church like the old missionaries who would take five months on a boat to arrive at their continent. She says, "The cell church helps us enter the jet age . . ."[40] Pastor César says:

> We know of many churches that have concentrated on numerous programs that don't contribute to the growth of the church and to the multiplication that God desires. For years we passed through the same problems until we understood that the only viable program that fulfilled God's purpose was cell ministry; we decided to pattern our entire church around this ministry. There is no other program that has captured our attention. Why? Because we are living in the twenty-first century.[41]

Some confuse the G-12 system with a system that competes with the cell group structure. This is not the case. Castellanos argues that only the cell structure will harvest thousands upon thousands of souls and convert church spectators into active members. The cell church, reasons Pastor Castellanos, is the only effective means to mobilize the entire church to win souls. He says, " . . . in a cell church, the senior pastor focuses on preaching and motivating the sheep to multiply."[42] The ministry of evangelism and discipleship is shared with the entire church through cell groups.

ICM almost strayed from the cell church vision. They became acquainted with a man who possessed an apostolic vision for planting churches. Castellanos prematurely adopted this man's vision as his own and wanted to begin opening new churches. ICM began training 200 pastors to plant new churches.[43]

At that time, César and Claudia Castellanos attended a church-planting seminar at Yoido Full Gospel Church. As Pastor César was listening to the speaker, the Spirit of God said to him, "You shouldn't do what all of these other seminar participants are planning on doing."[44] At the very same time, his wife, Claudia, was taking a workshop on saturation evangelism and the Spirit of God gave her the same message.

This decision was confirmed while listening to Cho on Sunday morning. Because of the crowds, some were forced to stand. The Lord spoke to Castellanos saying, "I've given you a vision, just like David Cho, to grow a huge church based on cell groups, and you are trying to introduce a new vision within the church!"[45] God clearly showed Pastor César that He didn't want him to plant dozens and dozens of small churches. Rather, God had given them a vision to start a huge cell church that would cover the entire city.

They had to go back to ICM and humble themselves before the 200 church planting pastors, admitting that they had erred in judgment. Castellanos asked for their forgiveness. But God blessed his obedience as this marked the period when the church skyrocketed from 1,400 cells to 4,000 cells and then in 1996 to 10,000 cells.

Planting new churches is not wrong. Church planting, in fact, is the most effective way to fulfill the great commission. ICM continues to plant churches all over the world today. Yet the church planting emphasis was leading ICM away from establishing a strong citywide cell church in Bogota.

Castellanos now tells his people, "The cell church vision is exciting. Don't stray from it. A cell church must have one vision. Don't try to take a little bit from each church. Love the cell church vision. Love the cell groups."[46]

IS A NEW MODEL THE SOLUTION?

Don't think that a new model will cure your church. You must also adopt the values of ICM, which include submission, time commitment, and a total dedication to holiness and spirituality. ICM talks much more about spiritual power, spiritual victories and spiritual liberation and relatively little about the model. Visitors become enamored with the model. You'll never get the same results as Bogota by simply copying a model without taking with you the values of the church.

God has given ICM the boldness to adjust and change. This is a lesson for all those entering G-12 ministry. Ask God for the power of creativity. Make adjustments according to your needs and don't get locked into one system. As soon as you find yourself asking the question, "What would such-and-such a church do?" you know that you need to spend more time before God, asking Him for wisdom to fit your situation.

THE HEART

OF THE CHURCH

It is 4:15 P.M. and the meeting started. Margaret has been attending for four weeks and has learned that people are not overly concerned about starting on time. Already, these people have become like family. She loves these one-hour meetings. They fit nicely into her schedule, and she even gets to eat with her new friends when the meeting is over.

Mary, the cell leader, begins with prayer. Singing follows. As a new Christian, Margaret appreciates the music and the help of the song sheets.

The lesson begins after 20 minutes, and Margaret recognizes many of the concepts because Pastor Castellanos preached on the passage last Sunday. Margaret doesn't feel threatened in the group because everyone is encouraged to participate. "How can I be sure that Jesus forgives me?" she asks. Mary lovingly points to 1 John 1:9 which reads, "If we confess our sins, he is faithful and just and will forgive us our sins and purify us from all unrighteousness."

The prayer time follows, and Margaret has a chance to ask for prayer for her second son who is struggling in school. Finally, an offering is taken and Mary, along with Joan the co-leader, counts the offering in front of the rest of the group. The money is placed inside a yellow envelope to be handed to the church treasurer on Sunday morning. The meeting concludes with prayer.

TYPICAL CELL GROUP

If you attend a cell group at ICM, your experience would resemble Margaret's.[1] Most cells at ICM have between six and nine people and include prayer, worship, lesson, and offering. Here's the schedule:

1. Preliminary activity (five minutes)
2. Introduction (ten minutes)
3. Cell lesson based on the Sunday morning sermon (30 minutes)
4. Application (five minutes)
5. Final activity (five minutes)
6. Offering and fill out the report (five minutes)

The cells are divided according to homogeneity. Although cells are now open to mixed groups (men, women, children), the majority of the cells fall into one of these categories: all male, all female, couples, young professional, youth, adolescent, or children.

EVANGELISM: THE FOCUS OF THE CELL

Pastor Castellanos insists that all the cell groups must be evangelistic. He remembers a time when those at ICM found cell members from within the church. Not anymore. Now they go outside the church to find the people. Castellanos exhorts his cell leaders to assume responsibility for their neighborhoods.

They use two dominant methods to evangelize in the cell. First, the cells place an empty chair in the middle, and the group prays for someone new to fill it. Second, the cells practice the principle called "the prayer of three." Each cell member begins praying for three non-Christian friends. As God answers prayer, these people are integrated into the cell. Evangelism, therefore, doesn't depend on the cell leader. His job, rather, is to mobilize each member to evangelize, which starts with prayer. Castellanos says, "If the leader of the cell group does all of the work, the group won't grow."[2]

THE ROLE OF THE CELL LEADER

At ICM, the cell leader is considered the pastor of the cell. Castellanos openly exhorts his cell leaders to remember they are pastors. The leader must visit each person in the cell group and get to know the personal details of his or her life. For this reason, all leaders at ICM receive instruction about the importance of visitation and how to do it.[3]

GOD'S PRESENCE IN THE CELL

Like most cell churches worldwide, ICM emphasizes similarity in its cell vision. All the cells will follow the same theme based on the Sunday morning sermon.[4] The Sunday morning message is transcribed and then distributed to the cell leaders.[5] The Word of God, then, takes on central significance in the cell. Castellanos exhorts his cell leaders not to stray from the Word of God and more specifically, the passage of Scripture preached on Sunday. Prophecy is not allowed within the cell group. ICM wants to avoid splinter groups and heresy at all costs.

The cells at ICM are spiritual cells. The goal of the cell group is to obtain the presence of God. I've heard messages at ICM relating the home cell group figuratively to the place where the Ark of the Covenant rested. Like the Old Testament temple that housed the Ark of the Covenant, so also God's Spirit dwells in the home cell group.[6] Fervent prayer is the chief means to maintain God's presence in the cell group.

ICM teaches that a cell group should meet weekly, rather than bimonthly or monthly. Castellanos says, "A monthly cell brings minimum life. You must meet once per week."[7] ICM does not encourage cells to rotate from house to house. They believe that a cell should have only one place to meet, so everyone knows where to go.[8]

MORE THAN ONE GROUP

There is a great difference between the number of cell groups and the number of cell leaders at ICM, since it's quite normal for a cell leader to lead more than one group. The goal, of course, is to raise-up leaders to take over the group, but in the process it's not uncommon for one leader to direct two or more small groups. Zealous leaders have plenty of room at ICM to serve.

I talked to Ricardo, a youth cell leader, who at the time led four cell groups and served as a "coach" for five more. While building his 12 disciples, Ricardo had to lead most of the groups. However, he sought to eventually delegate leadership of those cells to others.[9] Aware of the dangers of burnout, the young people now limit cell leaders to no more than two cell groups.[10]

EVERY MEMBER A LEADER

Margaret continued to grow spiritually as she attended her weekly cell group. She would have been content just attending her cell for years, but she soon learned from Mary, her cell leader, that everyone at ICM needed to begin the equipping track with the goal of becoming a cell leader. She began to hear about the groups of 12 and how Mary hoped to develop her into one of her 12 disciples. She became aware that it wasn't sufficient just to attend the cell group. She also needed to become a disciple of Jesus Christ, which means following Jesus and leading others to do the same.

THE G-12

SYSTEM

Mario received Jesus Christ at ICM six years ago. Jesus radically changed his life, and gave him a hunger to win others. He began to share the good news of Jesus Christ with his buddies. John, Mario's friend from elementary school, responded to the gospel message and began attending Mario's cell group. As John attended Mario's cell group and grew in his relationship with Jesus Christ, he heard about the need for further training. John attended a spiritual retreat, took Bible-oriented classes, and eventually opened his own cell group. Throughout this entire process, John continued to attend Mario's cell group. When John started his own cell group, he officially became one of Mario's 12 disciples, thus cementing their relationship even further. Now John is looking for his own disciples.

ORGANIZATIONAL CHART OF THE G-12

A G-12 group is not a cell group. Instead it is the place where cell leaders are led, nurtured, and supported. Every leader has a goal of developing his or her own G-12 group, just like Mario. All leaders, therefore, are members of a G-12 group and also seek to lead a G-12 group of their own. The ICM structure looks like this:

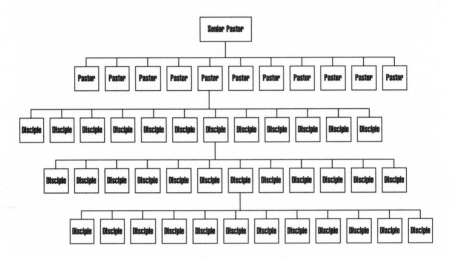

THREE MEETINGS

John meets on *Monday* in the home of Mario, his G-12 leader. John enjoys these meetings because he has weekly, personal contact with Mario and a chance to share about his cell group and his progress in finding his own 12 disciples. John also receives spiritual ministry and prayer from Mario and often an exhortation from God's Word. 11 other disciples of Mario are also present on Monday night.

On *Tuesday* night John leads his own open cell group. Like all cell leaders, John follows the weekly cell lesson, which is based on the Sunday morning sermon. John longs to see more non-Christians in his home cell group and tries to invite as many people as possible.

Then on *Thursday* night, John leads his own G-12 group. Only three people attend his Thursday night G-12 meeting because right now he only has three of his 12 disciples. He hopes to find the additional nine very soon. His three disciples came from his own cell group. Tim, for example, first started attending John's Tuesday night cell group nine months ago. John prayed with Tim to receive Christ and immediately Tim started the ICM training track: a three-day retreat, three-month school of leadership, and a second three-day retreat. When Tim began leading his own cell group, he then became "John's disciple" and thus began meeting every Thursday night with John in the G-12 group. Now Tim is looking for his own disciples, just like John.

The G-12 model at ICM requires three separate meetings for every leader (day and time of meetings vary):[1]

1. You meet with the one who is discipling you
2. You lead an open cell group
3. You meet with the 12 that you're discipling

Beyond the three basic core meetings at ICM, there is the congregational meeting (e.g., young people, women, etc.) and the celebration service on Sunday. Many have a summit meeting each week that consists of the entire network of disciples (the 12 of the 12 of the 12, etc. of the original cell leader).

DISCIPLESHIP IN HOMOGENEOUS CATEGORIES

All three of John's weekly meetings are comprised of males. John meets together with Mario on Monday night along with 11 other male disciples. Then on Tuesday night, John leads a men's cell group. On

Thursday, John meets with his three male disciples as John is under the men's homogeneous department.[2]

Pastor Castellanos has 12 male disciples and all other disciples flow from these 12 disciples. John's wife, Beatrice, is under the women's homogenous grouping that was established by Claudia Castellanos. John and Beatrice could have chosen to minister as a couple under the homogenous department called "couples." If they had chosen this option, they would have then discipled couples and led an open cell group designed for couples.

At ICM men disciple men, women disciple women, couples disciple couples, and youth disciple youth.

Since you find your "disciples" within your cell group, your cell group will most likely reflect one homogeneous flavor. These homogenous categories include men, women, couples, young professionals, young people, adolescents, and children. If you lead a male home cell group, most likely only men will attend (previously this was the rule at ICM, but more recently it's permissible to have heterogeneous cell groups under men's ministry). The same applies to the women's groups. Maintaining the same homogeneity makes it easier to find disciples.

When a Person Becomes a Disciple

Just what is a disciple? The most basic New Testament definition of a disciple is pupil or follower. Jesus chose 12 followers. At ICM, a disciple is a cell leader and a cell leader is a disciple. If you want to be a disciple and form part of the 12 of someone, you must also lead a cell group.

I once asked César Fajardo, "Can you call a person part of your 12 if the person has not yet opened a cell group?" César Fajardo wrote back saying, "It's clear that if someone isn't leading a cell group, he or she isn't a leader of anything and the G-12 groups are groups of leaders."[3]

Let me emphasize this last phrase: *G-12 groups are groups of leaders.* ICM is a cell church, so at ICM a disciple is a cell leader and a cell leader is a disciple. You might be a "disciple in process" while you're taking the training to become a cell leader. You're not, however, part of the "12" of someone until you're actually leading a cell group. César Castellanos says: ". . . all of the 12 must be there because of merit. They have to give birth to new cells, thus bearing fruit."[4] César Castellanos gives this instruction:

> You only choose your 12 after the person has borne fruit [opened a cell group]. If you choose too quickly [before opening a cell group] based on friendship or sympathy, it might turn out that the person never opens a cell, and thus you will never achieve your objective. The person who does not produce is hindering the conversion of thousands of people.[5]

Discipleship at ICM is not a static, ingrown activity. Since a disciple must lead a cell group, the concept of 12 is a method to multiply groups more rapidly. The goal is that each person in the church leads a cell group in order to be a true disciple. If the person refuses to lead a cell group, it's best to terminate the discipleship relationship.[6]

ICM has only two titles: discipler (leader of 12) and disciple (cell leader). They have eliminated cell church titles like district pastor, zone pastor and zone supervisor or section leader. The G-12 system continues to flow to the lowest levels, and everyone disciples through G-12 groups as well as evangelizing through open cell groups.

WHEN A G-12 LEADER STOPS LEADING
AN OPEN CELL GROUP

What happens when you've found your 12 disciples? Do you still need to lead an open cell group? Most leaders at ICM continue to lead an open cell until all of their 12 have also found 12. Take the example of John and Mario. Mario has already found his 12 disciples and meets on Monday night with John and 11 other disciples. Mario, even though he has found his 12, continues to lead an open cell group. Why? Because he knows that John only has three disciples, and Mario desires for John to find nine more.

So Mario channels the potential disciples from his open group to John's group. Mario does the same thing for his other 11 disciples who have not yet found their 12.

Mario's ultimate goal is that each of his 12 disciples finds 12 disciples and then Mario will have 144 disciples. When Mario has reached the number 144, he'll stop leading an open cell.[7]

When a G-12 leader reaches 144, he or she would be heavily involved in training future leaders, and thus it wouldn't be feasible to continue leading an open cell group. Many leaders who have reached this point (144) are teaching their own equipping tracks and thus are no longer depending on someone higher up the ladder to do the training (explained more in the next chapter).

EVERYONE A POTENTIAL LEADER AND SUPERVISOR

The original cell structure (often called the 5x5 system), developed by David Yonggi Cho of the Yoido Full Gospel Church, teaches that the church must *appoint* a supervisor to care for each cluster of five cell groups. In the 5x5 cell system, John could not have supervised (discipled) new cell leaders until he was asked to become a supervisor by a higher-level leader (e.g., a zone pastor). The title "supervisor" is an appointed position.

The G-12 model, in contrast, expects John like everyone else to become a supervisor (although ICM calls it a discipler). At ICM, it's not sufficient for John to simply lead a cell group. Rather, he must raise-up new cell leaders from his group and then supervise them through his own G-12 group.

In this system, every person is a potential leader and every leader is a potential supervisor. Everyone from the senior pastor to the kitchen worker is commissioned to find 12 disciples, primarily from among the new Christians.

It's amazing how many common people at ICM are actually supervising others. Willie, who drove us around in the van, had 45 cell groups under his care. He hoped to be supervising 250 cells within a year. We talked to a young girl who cleaned the floor, who supervised four cell groups. The phone operator for ICM had 80 cell groups under her care. Another security guard had already formed his G-12 group and was now seeking to form his group of 144. Castellanos says:

> We even have humble people who are handling large numbers
> of cells. Even the cleaning ladies have cell groups. Everyone
> has cells. Some have two, others seven, others 50, others many,
> many more. In order to become a part-time minister in our
> church, a person must have 250 cells. In order to become full-
> time in the church, a person must have 500.[8]

EVERYONE RECEIVES MINISTRY IN ORDER TO MINISTER

Billy Graham was once asked, "If you were a pastor, what strategy would you implement?" Billy Graham replied, "I would choose 12 people and transmit my life to them. I would then send them out to do the work."[9] The idea of transmitting life and ministering to the ministers is central to the G-12 system. In the normal, program-oriented church, about 40 people have direct access to the pastor. Through the G-12 model, the care system of the pastor is passed down to each one.[10]

Everyone who is leading a cell forms part of a G-12 group. If a person has not yet opened a cell group, he or she receives care from the open cell group leader. But the badge of honor at ICM is to form part of a G-12 group. Therefore everyone desires to enter the training process in order to become a cell leader and thus form part of a G-12 group.

We all know that the ministers need ministry in order to minister more effectively. When someone asks César Castellanos for counsel, the first question that he asks the person is: "Who is your leader?" The person answers: "I'm part of the 12 of the 12 of such-and-such a person."[11] Castellanos expects the G-12 leader to offer counsel and ministry to the cell leader before looking to anyone higher.[12]

THE SIGNIFICANCE OF THE NUMBER 12

"I believe the number seven would be better than 12 for my church in Juarez, Mexico," said the senior pastor. "Our houses are smaller than those of Bogota, and 12 is just too many for our context," he said to me. We batted around the idea concerning whether or not the number 12 was essential.

ICM believes strongly in the special significance of the number 12. They base this belief on that fact that God spoke clearly to pastor Castellanos in 1991 about the G-12 concept.[13] Pastor Castellanos also regularly preaches on the importance of the number 12. He references the fact that God chose 12 tribes of Israel (Genesis 35:22-26; Exodus 28:21), the Hebrew calendar has 12 months, Solomon had 12 governors (1 Kings 4:7), and Jesus chose 12 disciples (Luke 6:12-15).

Luis Salas, one of the 12 of Castellanos, says to his potential leaders, "The number 12 is your key to success. From this day onwards, you will dream and pray about the number 12. The most important thing that you can do is make disciples."[14]

MATERIAL USED IN THE G-12 MEETING

Sometimes, Mario teaches his disciples a message passed down from César Castellanos. Until his recent move to Miami, Pastor Castellanos met with his 12 on a weekly basis. His 12 took fervent notes of the content of that meeting and passed the message down to their disciples. What was learned from the senior pastor was then passed down to the entire leadership structure through the G-12 system.[15]

It's my observation, however, that the content of most G-12 meetings at ICM depend on the G-12 leader and what he or she receives directly from the Lord.[16] Mario, for example, begins his G-12 meeting asking each disciple to share his personal needs. "I'm struggling in my marriage," says John. "Please pray for me." Those present lay hands on John, praying that Jesus would heal his marriage. After praying for each disciple, Mario says, "Now I'd like each of you to share what happened in your cell group and G-12 group during the past week." This has been a tough week for John since only three people attended his cell group and only one disciple attended his G-12 group meeting. "Keep on pressing on, John," exhorts Mario. "I've been there. Make sure you call your disciples this week and keep on inviting new people to your cell group," Mario says.

Then Mario reminds his disciples about the men's evangelistic rally in three months. "This is going to be a huge event. We've rented the indoor stadium, and we all need to be praying. Remember also that in one month we're going to invite our wives and families to meet with us at the retreat center."

Normally Mario edifies his leaders through a passage from God's Word, and he tries to limit his G-12 meeting to one hour.

THE PLACE TO MEET WITH THE 12

Mario, like most G-12 leaders, opens his home for the G-12 meetings. However, I've seen G-12 meetings in the church building after a celebration service or in an isolated corner outside the sanctuary. G-12 groups can meet in restaurants, classrooms, or wherever. By far the most common meeting place is in the home.

SUMMIT MEETINGS

When each of Mario's disciples has found his 12, Mario can then claim to have 144 disciples. That number could continue to grow as the 144 make disciples (thus giving Mario grandchildren and great grandchildren).

As a G-12 network grows to 144 disciples, degeneration of vision and quality can occur. The further away a disciple is from the original discipler, the higher the degeneration. ICM, therefore, has created summit meetings to maintain a high standard of quality control.

At the summit meeting, the network leaders gather their entire network of disciples on a regular basis. Like Mario, some G-12 leaders gather their network on a bimonthly basis. Others meet once a month, and still others meet every week.

GROWING AS A DISCIPLE

John has not yet arrived at spiritual maturity. He still struggles in his marriage, for example. Yet, since completing the equipping track and becoming actively involved in the ministry, he is growing daily. He feels responsible to exemplify the life of Christ to his disciples, so he personally studies the Word and prays continually. When he has questions and doubts, he knows that he can approach Mario at any time, and that he will receive answers. At times John marvels at how completely his life has changed since hearing Mario's testimony six years ago. He's so thankful to be Mario's disciple, but even more important to be a disciple of Jesus Christ.

THE TRAINING SUCCESS
OF ICM

The drug war culture of Colombia has created many enemies — even among family members. One young man entered ICM filled with the fruits of bitterness that were sown in his own home. He hated his father. Fierce anger controlled him, even after receiving Jesus Christ. This man needed soul therapy — a "rotor-rooter" cleansing deep within the confines of his soul. He entered the equipping track at ICM, and Jesus transformed him. Afterwards, he was able to go to his father and confess the hate and bitterness that controlled him. As Jesus healed him, he became one of the key instruments in Bogota to reach men for Jesus Christ.[1] Castellanos says: "There are many leaders and pastors who want to have a powerful ministry, but because of inner wounds, they are never very productive. These wounds must first be healed."[2]

"What is your opinion of the International Charismatic Mission," I asked a non-Christian taxi driver in Bogota, as he drove me to the church. "Well, I don't attend the church," he began, "but I do know many people who have been changed through that church."[3]

Every cell church has some kind of an equipping system, but not every equipping track is created equal. ICM has created an equipping track that is worth noting. It resembles a leadership development machine that stirs people to stand-up and pay attention. ICM has developed a pattern to set people free and equip leaders rapidly and thoroughly.

The Evolution of Leadership Training at ICM

Pastor Castellanos was so enthusiastic about Yoido Full Gospel Church after his initial visit that he tried to copy its training system. ICM's Bible Institute offered courses in hermeneutics, homiletics, eschatology, false cults, Old Testament and New Testament theology, and all the courses the found in the Bible college at the Korean church.

ICM's Bible institute aimed to train people to lead a cell group in two years and held classes every day of the week. Yoido Full Gospel Church does not require that people graduate from their college to lead a cell group, but ICM required that all future leaders complete their Bible institute.

As the leadership inspected the fruit, they acknowledged their dismal failure.[4] If 70 began the institute training, 15 finished. Worse yet, after two years many of the potential cell leaders had lost contact with their non-Christian friends. They no longer desired to evangelize after such a long absence from ministry. After two years, the students suddenly felt that they needed more training to minister properly. ICM only added 70 cell groups in the seven years of following the Bible institute model.[5]

Pastor Castellanos, a pragmatist at heart, saw the handwriting on the wall. He cried out to God saying, "Father, give me a new method. You know that we've been trying to develop leaders, but we've lacked something. I feel like I'm facing a giant brick wall. Help me."[6]

God answered Castellano's prayers and showed him how to train potential leaders more effectively and quickly. ICM began a pilot project called the School of Leadership, which allows the potential cell leaders to stay in the battle of winning a lost world while taking basic courses. The leadership school focuses on three areas: doctrine, vision of the church, and cell ministry. The crowning jewel of ICM training is a three-day retreat that releases the new convert from the chains of past bondage.

EVERYONE RAPIDLY TRAINED FOR CELL LEADERSHIP

With the new training focus, ICM now prepares new converts very quickly for cell leadership. Castellanos says, "Here lies the secret. We've discovered how to train each person rapidly . . . It takes us more or less six months from their conversion until they become a cell leader."[7] Although the average time to become a cell leader at ICM is six months, Luis Salas, one of the 12 of Castellanos, prepares his new leaders in four to five months. On the other hand, César Fajardo recommends between six to eight months.[8]

Another secret behind the training miracle at ICM is that entering the equipping track is the standard for everyone. Castellanos says, "Until we learned this, leadership training was optional. We asked the people if they wanted to be trained. With this mentality, it was difficult to train even a small group of 30 to 40 people. But God showed me that the training wasn't optional."[9] If a person wants to become part of ICM, he or she must enter the equipping track. Those who refuse to enter the ICM equipping track do not blend in at ICM.

THE ICM EQUIPPING TRACK

Referring to long-term cell multiplication, Luis Salas said, " . . . unless you're ready to prepare leaders, you'll have nothing to show for it."[10] Rapid multiplication requires systematic leadership training. The following steps outline the official process for every new convert. Flexibility, however, reigns. For example, many new believers do not start with the Encounter Retreat. Rather, they immediately enter the School of Leadership and only later attend an Encounter Retreat. Two reasons for this include: lack of money to pay for the retreat and hesitancy to immediately attend a charismatic gathering. The young people, among whom the training system was first tested, are more consistent in following the precise order.

Step One: Initial Follow-up
During the celebration services (entire gathered church on Sunday) or congregational service (one of the homogeneous groupings), the speaker always gives an invitation to receive Jesus Christ.[11] Large numbers respond and are gathered into a separate room after the service. Trained workers present the gospel once again in a crystal clear manner.

Then the counselors give individual attention to each convert. These counselors are chosen from the G-12 networks of each homogeneous ministry on a rotating basis.

During the consolidation time, the counselors ask for prayer requests. The counselor then prays for the new convert and asks him to record his personal information on a card. Another counselor will then confirm the information on the card: "Okay, so you're name is _____ and you live where?"

After this, the cards are distributed to the different homogeneous departments (men, women, couples, young professionals, young people, adolescents, and children) for ongoing follow-up and care by a cell group. For example, César Fajardo has 12 disciples under him in the youth ministry. Each of his disciples takes one month out of the year to follow-up the new converts. When it's Freddy Rodriguez's turn to take the follow-up cards, he will receive all the cards designated for young people from the Sunday celebration service as well as the young people service on Saturday night. Freddy will distribute the cards among his 12 disciples. His 12 will work with their 12 and on down the line. Freddy's G-12 leaders (and their G-12 leaders) will call the new people by telephone within 48 hours.

This same process is repeated among the men, women, couples, young professionals, adolescents, and children. G-12 leaders from each homogeneous department will call on Monday and ask the new contacts about particular prayer requests which were written on the card. "How is your mother? We're praying for her. Can we visit you?" That same week visitation takes place with the goal of landing the new person in a cell group. Follow-up is not complete until the new convert is regularly attending a cell group.

Step Two: Life in the Cell
The new person begins the Christian life in a cell group. Patricia, a divorced mother of three children, received Jesus on Sunday morning at ICM. On Monday, Joanne, the leader of a cell for women, called Patricia, inviting her to attend her cell group on Wednesday afternoon. Joanne even offered to give Patricia a ride to the cell. Although Patricia felt nervous the first time in Joanne's cell, she soon began to treasure the times of personal sharing and knows that she will always find a safe haven in Joanne's cell group. Joanne calls Patricia often.

It wasn't long before Patricia heard about a three-day retreat called an "Encounter Retreat." Joanne encouraged her to attend and even offered to accompany her. "Okay, Lord, if this is the next step, I'll do it," Patricia whispered to God. Joanne informed her that she must first take three preparatory lessons before attending the retreat.

Step Three: Pre-Encounter

Before attending an Encounter Retreat new believers are required to complete three of the six Navigators books on the basics of the Christian life. These lessons include: New Life in Christ, Walking with Christ, and Fellowship with Christ. Each lesson is covered in one weekly session, so this phase lasts for three weeks. These classes are offered in the church and dictated by a trained teacher within the women's homogeneous group.[12]

Castellanos writes, "The person who accepts the Lord goes through what we call the Pre-Encounter period; it's a preparation period . . . So when they arrive at the retreat, they have a few foundations."[13] In these sessions, they teach the new converts the ABC's of the Christian life in order to prepare them for the Encounter Retreat.

Step Four: Encounter Retreat

Many who accept Jesus Christ at ICM are filled with hurts, dysfunctional behavior, and sinful patterns from a life controlled by the prince of darkness. In the past, ICM believed that with the simple act of lifting up a hand and saying, "I accept Jesus," the convert would change.

They soon realized that "accepting Jesus" was only the first step. They understood that those who "accepted Jesus" needed a time of drawing nigh to God. They recognized the necessity for each new believer to experience an encounter with Jesus.[14] Now ICM believes that a three-day Encounter Retreat is equal to one whole year of attending the church for a new believer.[15]

The Encounter Retreat takes place within every homogeneous grouping (men, women, couples, professionals, youth, adolescents, and children). Ralph Neighbour and I attended an Encounter weekend among the young professionals at a rustic, spacious motel in the country. Some 80 young professionals were present.

If the Encounter Retreat happens among the women's homogeneous group, only women attend. The same is true for the men's homogeneous group. The exception is with the couple's ministry. Within this category, there are three Encounter Retreats. The first one is for women, the second for men, and the final retreat brings the couples together. Among the couples, ICM always places the women's Encounter first, to stir an attitude of repentance and prayer, following the principle of 1 Peter 3:1-6.

Among the young people alone, more than 500 people attend six to eight Encounter Retreats every weekend.[16]

Normally, between 70-120 people attend a retreat. An Encounter Retreat starts on Friday evening and finishes late Sunday afternoon. Everyone pays his or her own fee for the event. These retreats occur at designated retreat centers (e.g., ranch home, hotel, farm house) throughout Bogota. ICM purposely takes the participants away from the city and routine schedules, so that God can work more powerfully. ICM resists the notion that an Encounter can take place in the church, since it's too near the hustle and bustle of daily chores and activity.[17]

One month before the Encounter Retreat takes place, the leaders and the corresponding network of disciples engage in fervent prayer, spiritual warfare, and even fasting for those who will attend. ICM realizes that an Encounter Retreat is first and foremost a spiritual battle for the participants.[18]

During the Encounter, each person receives concentrated teaching about liberation from sin, the sanctified life, and the power of the

Holy Spirit. Castellanos says, "We minister to them assurance of salvation, inner healing, deliverance, and fullness of the Holy Spirit. When a person leaves the Encounter, the miracle has already taken place!"[19] My Encounter experience confirmed this. We noted a healthy balance between seminar teaching and personal ministry. The young professionals dedicated the morning to teaching and afternoon to personal ministry.

The Encounter Retreat deals with four areas in the person's life. First, there is teaching on the *security of salvation.* ICM wants to make sure that regeneration has taken place, and that the new convert has experienced God, rather than simply repeating the "sinner's prayer." Often, a person will truly receive Christ for the first time during an Encounter.[20]

Second, the participants experience *liberation and inner healing.* Designated leaders teach the people the true meaning of repentance and how to live in broken surrender before God. Often during an Encounter Retreat, those attending begin to pray, confess their sins, and even cry out to God with wailing and petitions.

The Encounter leaders also instruct the new converts concerning Christ's forgiveness and the believer's new position in Him. Often new Christians don't know how to forgive, nor to be forgiven. Many new Christians feel unworthy of receiving God's love. ICM teaches that Jesus Christ is vitally concerned about each person and that Christ wants to heal every sin and scar of the past.[21]

Castellanos believes that when a person fails to bear fruit, it is a symptom of some adverse force operating within. Hindrances might include: rejection in childhood, traumatic moments during adolescent years, sinful relationships, involvement in the occult, conflictive family relationships, curses, and other such occurrences.[22] In the Encounter Retreat, ICM uses a diagnostic tool to determine the roots of generational curses.

Often people don't know that they're under the judgment of God because of their sin. In the Encounter Retreat, past sins are revealed and confessed, allowing liberation to occur.[23] The three-day retreat, then, is a time to receive healing from past bondage.

Third, the Encounter Retreat is a time to receive the *fullness of the Spirit of God.* ICM believes that the evidence of tongues accompanies the baptism of the Holy Spirit. Most people, therefore, speak in tongues at an Encounter Retreat. ICM encourages believers to speak in tongues during their private prayer life. In the celebration services at ICM, however, the manifestation of tongues must include a proper interpretation.[24]

Fourth, the new believer receives teaching about the *vision of ICM.*[25] Those attending hear about ICM's plans to reach an entire nation through the cell church philosophy and how each one of them can actively participate.

Often there is a campfire, and those attending write a letter about their old life. Then they throw the letter into the fire, symbolically demonstrating that the old life has passed, and the new life in Christ has now arrived. Afterwards, there is joyful singing and praise.

Apart from the intense teaching and ministry times, Encounter Retreats also emphasize fun and relaxation. Sports, food, and fellowship make it easy for new friendships to develop.[26]

Step Five: Post-Encounter

The Post-Encounter takes place immediately after the Encounter Retreat. The final three Navigator lessons are offered during the Post-Encounter time. These three lessons are: Foundations of the Faith, Growing in Christian Service, and Christian Character.[27] The Post-Encounter prepares the new believer to enter the School of Leadership. Before ICM implemented the Post-Encounter, many people left the church immediately after attending the Encounter

Retreat. ICM eventually realized that it was a counterattack from Satan. After implementing the Post-Encounter lessons, ICM has seen its retention rate dramatically increase.[28]

Step Six: School of Leadership

After the Post-Encounter teaching, the young believer attends the yearlong School of Leadership. There is an immediate bridge between the two, so that those attending the retreat and Post-Encounter teaching will enter the School of Leadership.[29]

The School of Leadership is a two-hour weekly class that takes place among the different homogeneous groups. The student attends only one class per week, not one per day as in the old system. Normally, there are at least fifty students per class.[30] The classes require more than attendance and listening to a teacher. Each student must participate and apply the lessons.[31] Among the young people alone, more than 7,000 people were taking the School of Leadership during the first semester of 1999.[32]

César Castellanos has written a book for each semester. *Encounter One* (first semester) covers God's purpose for mankind, man's sinful condition, the person of Jesus Christ and the uniqueness of Christianity. *Encounter Two* (second semester) deals with the cross of Jesus Christ. *Encounter Three* (third semester) teaches baptism, the devotional life, authority of the Scriptures and the doctrine of the Holy Spirit.[33] Another manual, *C.A.F.E. 2000* (a compilation of cell leadership training material), is taught alongside the Encounter manuals in order to prepare the person to lead a cell group.

Step Seven: Second Encounter Retreat

This second retreat is designed to reinforce the commitments made at the first retreat and to instill final principles in the potential leader before he or she launches a cell group.[34] The second retreat normally occurs after the first semester of the School of Leadership, immediately before the person starts leading his or her cell group.

The second Encounter Retreat that I attended included teaching on our position in Christ, victory over sin and personal liberation. It's a time to capture the vision of the church and renew one's faith.

Step Eight: Lead a Cell Group

Again, there is no need to finish the entire School of Leadership before opening a cell group. Many, in fact, lead an open cell before attending a second Encounter Retreat. Some leaders, like Luis Salas, won't allow anyone to enter the second semester of the School of Leadership unless they're leading a cell group. It's also clear that you can't graduate from the third semester of the School of Leadership without leading a cell group.

Step Nine: More in-depth Teaching

For a long time ICM used Theological Education by Extension (called FLET) for higher-level leadership training.[35] They now offer higher-level training based on a series of books called "Firm as a Rock," authored by Pastor César Castellanos.[36]

Step Ten: School of Teachers

In the initial stages of the equipping track, Pastor Castellanos and his original 12 disciples taught the leadership training courses. The explosive growth of the church, however, demanded an ever-broadening pool of teachers.

The School of Teachers is a course designed to train potential teachers to teach in the school of leadership. These potential teachers are taught using a book called Guia del Maestro [Teacher's Guide], which takes them once again through the *Encounter* books, but this time with an emphasis on how to teach in a systematic way.

They are taught the methodology of teaching skills, and then more specifically how to apply the teaching to the lives of their students. ICM normally trains more than 100 people each semester to become teachers in the School of Leadership. The majority of these people are already professionals.

THE GOAL: TRANSFORMATION

Everything done at ICM is aimed at ultimately presenting people complete in Christ. Hugo is just another story of supernatural transformation.

"I used to spend the night on this piece of cement, huddled up against that wall," said Hugo. "My life was so controlled by drugs that I walked about in a daze and slept on the streets of Bogota all night. Then Jesus saved me."

Hugo reminded me of the story of Jesus and the demon-possessed man from Gerasenes. We read, "When they came to Jesus, they found the man from whom the demons had gone out, sitting at Jesus' feet, dressed and in his right mind; and they were afraid. So the man went away and told all over town how much Jesus had done for him" (Luke 8:35, 39).

As I spent time with Hugo, I saw first-hand how God is transforming the life of a Colombian drug addict. Hugo has now passed through each step of the equipping track at ICM, and I can testify that he is once again "in his right mind."

6

BE FRUITFUL
AND MULTIPLY

During one of my visits to ICM, I attended an evening cell group in an isolated neighborhood. After the meeting, I had to walk over a mile in the blackness of night to catch a bus. Fear gripped me when I saw a group of men walking behind me on the dirt road. I tried to ignore the fact that Colombia's murder rate is eight times higher than that of the U.S.[1]

Colombia has a tarnished reputation from the years of violence and corruption that has plagued this nation. The International Charismatic Mission, however, is committed to transforming Colombia. César once told me, "We are debtors to the world."[2] ICM plans to change Colombia through the creation of a powerful cell church that is continually multiplying cell groups. Pastor Castellanos says, "God wants your church to be fruitful and multiply. He desires your church to grow so large that you'll have an impact on the entire nation."[3]

ICM believes that multiplication gives authority — political and otherwise. The church has grown so rapidly that they now can exert influence in government circles because of the thousands upon thousands of changed lives that are released into society. ICM is also actively involved in the political process, and its regular radio and television programs help reprogram Colombian society. The key to it all is multiplication.

God's Mandate to Multiply

According to Castellanos, God is extremely interested in multiplication because He is the God of multiplication. From the very first chapter of Genesis, we read about God's vision for multiplication: "God blessed mankind saying, 'Be fruitful and increase [multiply] in number; fill the earth and subdue it. Rule over the fish of the sea and the birds of the air and over every living creature that moves on the ground'" (Gen. 1:28).

In a similar fashion, God blessed Abraham at the age of 99 saying, "I will confirm my covenant between me and you and will greatly increase [multiply] your numbers" (Gen. 17:2). Jesus commands the same type of fruitfulness in John 15:8: "This is to my Father's glory, that you bear much fruit, showing yourselves to be my disciples." At the end of His ministry, Jesus commanded this same type of fruitfulness of His disciples: "All authority in heaven and on earth has been given to me. Therefore go and make disciples of all nations, baptizing them in the name of the Father and of the Son and of the Holy Spirit" (Matt. 28:18-19). ICM believes that the only viable way to conquer an entire city is through the multiplication of cell groups.[4]

FRUITFULNESS AND HOLINESS

Pastor Castellanos quickly points out that God is interested in numbers and holiness. These two themes run together. In Castellano's mind, fruitfulness in multiplication is a direct result of personal holiness. Multiplication cannot come through unholy servants. "Get right with God and He will multiply your cell group" is the underlying exhortation.

Adam and Eve lost their authority because they lost their holiness. Pastor Castellanos says, "When there is sin, the cell group will fall. If someone is living with someone outside of marriage you must not allow such a person to lead a cell group. Holiness must begin with the leader."[5] Claudia Castellanos says that in order to multiply cell groups you have to: obey the Word of God, be committed to holiness, have a healed heart and receive liberation.[6]

THE SPIRIT OF AUTHORITY

All authority has been granted to Jesus Christ. When He sent His 12 disciples into the world to make new disciples, He gave them His authority. Christ demonstrated His authority while on earth. He didn't say to the demons, "Will you please leave?" No, He commanded them to leave.

Some people in cell ministry say, "Lord, if it's Your will, I'll multiply my cell group." God wants you to know that it is His will. Receive the authority of Jesus Christ to be fruitful and multiply.

Luis Salas, one of the 12 of César Castellanos, led a conference at our church (the Republic Church) in November 1998. Luis was very direct with our people. He told us that when a leader says, "I can't multiply my group," he or she is failing to trust the authority and power of God, thus sinning against God. His message to our church was, "You can multiply your cell because God is the God of multiplication, and He will give you the power." The first thing that Luis Salas asked us to do as a church was to take down the banners that said, "Our goal: 100 cell groups" and to replace it with a new banner that said, "Our goal: 300 cell groups."[7]

WILLINGNESS TO MULTIPLY CELL GROUPS

The G-12 philosophy is primarily a vehicle to multiply groups more rapidly. Instead of waiting for an entire cell group to divide in two groups, this concept compels each member to enter the training process in order to eventually lead a cell group. Cell leaders actively look for cell members to lead new cell groups, thus becoming disciples in the process.

In this system, every cell member is a potential cell leader, but even more importantly, every cell member is a potential leader of cell leaders. The leader of a cell group that has developed another leader immediately becomes an overseer. Thus, the G-12 model avoids "relationship breaks" once a group multiplies. Cell leaders supervise the groups they multiply. The G-12 model provides a simpler, more natural structure that depends less on top leadership and more on leadership at the grass-roots level. Yet, it's also true that any church implementing the G-12 model must already possess a red-hot desire for cell multiplication to receive the full benefits.

Some cell ministries under-emphasize cell multiplication. "I don't want to promote numbers," some think. "It would be presuming on God to set goals for cell multiplication." Others say, "When my cell is healthy enough, it will just naturally multiply." While close-knit fellowship is a treasured value in the cell church, so often "communion" becomes cliquey fellowship if not guarded carefully. Cell members rarely want to multiply their cells. We're naturally more comfortable sharing our prayer requests with people we know. I admire the fact that ICM is willing to take risks in order to reach people for Jesus Christ.

CLASSIC MULTIPLICATION VERSUS G-12 MULTIPLICATION

The popular method of cell multiplication is mother-daughter multiplication, in which an existing cell group oversees the creation of a daughter cell by providing people, leadership and a measure of personal care. A group is formed from within the parent cell and sent forth to form a daughter cell. The daughter cell becomes a separate, independent cell group and is not directly supervised by the parent cell (this is the role of supervisors, zone pastors, etc.). This is the most frequently used method of cell multiplication.

In the G-12 model, each member of the group is asked to start his or her own cell, either separately or with one or two others from the parent cell. When the cell member becomes a cell leader, he continues to meet with his original cell leader, either in the normal cell group (Bethany World Prayer Center) or in a separate discipleship meeting (International Charismatic Mission).

MULTIPLICATION HAPPENS WITHOUT DIVISION

In mother-daughter multiplication, the group divides into two groups and relationships are generally severed. There is always the possibility of contact, but usually the new group comes under the supervision of another leader (i.e., an appointed supervisor). In the G-12 model, the parent cell leader continues to supervise and care for the new cell leader.

Multiplication without division is somewhat of a misnomer at ICM. At ICM, the new cell leader does not return each week to the parent cell. Rather, the parent cell leader meets with the new cell leader at another time during the week in a G-12 group. This makes sense because a normal cell doesn't provide the same spiritual meat for a new cell leader.

On the other hand, Bethany World Prayer Center in Baker, Louisiana asks each new leader to attend the parent cell, thus maintaining the link between parent cell and daughter cell. (The parent cell leader is encouraged, but not required, to meet with the new leader on other occasions as well.)

Multiplication without division is best defined as a continual relationship between parent cell leader and leader of the new cell, whether that relationship is maintained in the parent cell or in another meeting during the week. Mike Atkins, former senior pastor of the Church of the Nations, writes: "This approach allows for cell members to continue strengthening relationships, transparency and intimacy while at the same time being actively involved in leadership and leadership development."[8]

It is wise for the parent cell leader to invite the new cell leader to continue attending the parent cell. This takes away the sting of "division" and separation — especially during the first few months. Over time, however, the new leader begins to develop new relationships in the daughter cell and often doesn't feel the same need to return each week to the parent cell.

However, under all circumstances, the parent cell leader must maintain close contact with the new cell leader, whether that entails a return to the parent cell each week or an occasional separate meeting between the two.

LEADERSHIP REWARDS FOR MULTIPLICATION

Successful leadership is clearly measured at ICM. Successful leaders are those who have planted a number of new groups, have raised up new leaders to lead other groups and are now leaders of leaders. If someone has been successful in doing this and is now training leaders, that person receives a promotion in the church. To qualify for a part-time staff position at ICM, a leader must multiply his or her cell group 250 times. A full-time position is reserved for those who have multiplied their cell group 500 times.

THE KEY TO CELL MULTIPLICATION: LEADERSHIP

"You just can't let anybody lead a cell group, can you?" one seminar participant asked me. She had misunderstood my talk on cell multiplication at ICM and didn't take into account the leadership training process. I quickly corrected her misunderstanding, saying that at ICM, every potential leader must pass through the six-month training process. While cell multiplication motivates the process, the key to success is leadership development. It takes great skill to move a person from cell membership to cell leadership.

If a cell group does not multiply at ICM, the responsibility is placed on the leader.[9] ICM will often change the leadership of a stagnated group in order to breathe new life into it. Several leaders told me that it was a "sin" to close an existing cell group. For this reason, ICM concentrates on leadership development and training.

LIMITS TO RAPID MULTIPLICATION

ICM fulfilled the amazing feat of multiplying from less than 5,000 cells in early 1996 to 10,600 cells by the end of 1996. Then they bit off more than they could chew. They set the goal of 30,000 for 1997. Huge banners proclaimed this goal to all those entering the church. Under pressure, they multiplied groups quickly to reach the goal, but many of the new cells were weak and "non-existent"(cells only on paper). ICM didn't reach its goal for 1997 and only reached 24,000 cells in 1998.

Yet, even that number left much to be desired. In 1999 ICM performed house cleaning. They combined many of the weak, lifeless cells to form stronger cells. They made a new norm that a cell had to have six people to officially be called a cell group. In March 1999, they reduced the number of cells from 24,000 to 18,000.[10] By September 1999, this number increased back up to 20,000.

ICM had to admit that they multiplied cells too rapidly. In the cell church, there is a time for consolidation. The multiplication of weak cells can create problems in the long run, and ICM wisely dealt with that reality. After consolidating many weak cell groups, one of the 12 of César wrote me saying, "Don't look at the number as much as the quality of the cell groups. The quality will produce the fruit."[11]

EXAMPLES OF DIFFERENT LEVELS OF CELL LEADERSHIP

To illustrate multiplication at ICM, I've chosen a wide range of examples that represent several different stages of cell group multiplication. Carlos, the taxi driver, revealed that he was a member of a cell at ICM, but not a cell leader. Javier slowly entered the rhythm of cell multiplication at ICM, but now supervises two cell groups. Daniel, a youth leader has progressed since receiving Jesus Christ in 1995 and now oversees 35 cell groups. Luis Salas (600 cells) and Freddy Rodriguez (1,500 cells) are known throughout the church as exceptional examples of cell group multiplication.

Carlos, the Taxi Driver: Zero Cell Groups
Carlos, a taxi driver in Bogota, picked up my friend and me on our way to the young people's service. He heard us talking about ICM and then revealed that he also attended ICM.

I asked him how he heard about ICM. "I was invited by a friend to attend a cell group," he told us. "From there I attended a Saturday night young people's service where I received Jesus Christ."[12] Carlos had already been baptized and was in his second semester of the School of Leadership but had not yet attended an Encounter Retreat. He understood the goals of ICM, yet Carlos is an example of someone who had not entered the heart of the ICM vision, which is cell leadership. He understood the importance of cell group ministry but has not taken the necessary steps to enter into it.

Javier: Two Cell Groups

My acquaintance with Javier began during my first visit to ICM in 1996. Each subsequent year, I spent time with Javier and noted his slow but steady progress.[13]

Javier was born in 1964 in Bogota. The youngest in a family of seven, he felt pressure to measure-up to the ideals of his stern father. "My father beat me," he told me. "I faced additional pressure because my sisters achieved high marks in school and eventually became civil engineers like my father." To cope, Javier found relief in alcohol. By the age of 16, Javier was an alcoholic who found his manhood by roaming with the wrong crowd and taking drugs.

In 1986, he entered the university to study civil engineering. He continued drinking at the time, although only during the summer. He says, "By my third year in university 'the spirit of destruction' took over me and I became a total addict." Javier wandered about, trapped in a maze of drugs, sex and alcohol. "I woke up one day and realized that I hadn't attended the university for two weeks, so I decided to kill myself. I took 90 pills." Javier's sister rescued him, and even though he escaped the jaws of death, within months, he was once again enslaved by the same vices.

This time, to support his drug habit, he resorted to robbing from his own family. They banished Javier from their home. He says, "From 1991 to 1995, I slept in bus stops, at clinics and at friends' houses. Sometimes I wouldn't sleep for days because of the drugs. Other nights I would sleep on the doorstep of my parent's home. I brought great shame to my family, as my neighbors saw my terrible condition."

Javier became acquainted with ICM through the all-night prayer meetings. As he searched for drugs and a place to stay, he often went to ICM. "I passed by ICM to receive food, money and care," he told me. "I sensed the love of God, even though I didn't know Jesus." At times, Pastor Castellanos would even pray for him in his drug-ridden state.

In December 1995, he cried out to God saying, "I want to leave this life of drugs, but I can't do it myself." Although Javier was not entirely healed from his sinful past, Jesus began to work slowly in his life, and he began attending ICM in 1996. As I spent time with Javier on my first three visits, he confessed his continuing struggle with fornication, which hindered him from entering into the ICM vision.

God is a powerful God and by the end of 1998, He helped Javier break free from sexual sins. When I met Javier in 1999, he was a transformed person. At that time, Javier had passed through an Encounter Retreat and the entire School of Leadership. Javier now forms part of a G-12 group (one of the 144 of César Castellanos) and has found two of his own 12 disciples.

Daniel: 35 Cell Groups

"Is that a cell group?" I asked. The group seemed strange since it was meeting outside the indoor stadium right before the young people's service on Saturday night. I talked to the leader of the group afterwards. The leader introduced himself as Daniel, one of the 144 of Freddy Rodriquez. "This was an open cell meeting," Daniel informed me. I have my G-12 meeting at 2 P.M. on Saturday.

Daniel first attended ICM in 1995 and accepted Jesus at a Saturday night young people's service. Jesus saved him from a life of drugs and worldly dealings. Soon after receiving Jesus Christ, he attended an Encounter Retreat, School of Leadership, Second Encounter, and then opened his cell group and began to look for his 12.

Daniel is now a full-time employee for ICM, working in the radio ministry. In addition to working full-time for the church, Daniel continues to actively build his network of disciples. Daniel has already found his 12 disciples who are now seeking their 12 disciples. At this point, Daniel has 35 cell groups under him (some of his 12 have already found their disciples who have opened cell groups).

Luis Salas: 600 Cell Groups

In January 1996, Luis Salas began his first cell group under the direction of César Castellanos. Just over three years later, Luis had multiplied the one cell to over 600 cells. How did he do it? The following characteristics will give you a clue.

1. Becoming a Friend. "You first have to make them your friend," Luis told me. He teaches his new leaders to gather their friends together in order to start cell groups.[14] "You have to enter into their problems. You have to be with them," Luis teaches. Like Jesus, Luis is willing to make friends with people and in the process convert them into his followers. The saying is true: "People don't care how much you know until they know how much you care."

2. Zeal for Visitation. Luis Salas believes that a vital key in cell group growth and multiplication is personal visitation. He counsels those under him to make immediate contact with newcomers. "I don't stay more than one-half hour per visit," he told us. He realizes that people have other commitments and appreciate someone who respects their time.

3. Seeing the Diamonds in the Rough. When Salas held a cell seminar in our church in Quito, Ecuador, he constantly told us to look at each member in the cell as diamonds in the rough. "See each person in your cell group as a potential leader," was practically the theme of the entire seminar. After the seminar, I saw each member of my own cell group in a new light. Previously, I saw Aldo as an obstruction to my own cell group. "He's so gruff," I thought. "Others must be disturbed by him." But after hearing Salas, I saw Aldo's potential for the first time and encouraged him to enter the equipping track.

4. Passion for Training. Luis knows that the only way to fulfill his goals is to train new leaders. Therefore, he is constantly looking for emerging leaders and then training them. His courses in the School of Leadership are always full.

5. Spiritual Authority. Luis repeatedly told us that his people respect him because they've seen God working in his life. They see him as a model of faith, and they want to follow that model. They know that God has provided for him in desperate times, and thus his authority is real and living. Luis Salas also derives authority from his example as a family man. He has four small children running around the house. Although Salas leads over 600 cells groups, he still maintains a full-time job as a computer systems analyst. He is an exception to the rule. (Usually after 500 cells, a person becomes a full-time employee of ICM.)[15]

Freddy Rodríguez: 1,500 Cell Groups

Before 1987, Freddy lacked hope and confidence. His life centered on drugs and alcohol. His family had separated and his father, who lived in the United States, wanted nothing to do with him. In this state of loneliness and frustration, Freddy received Jesus at ICM in 1987 and became one of the 12 disciples of César Fajardo. At that time there were only 60 people in the young people's group.

Within three years Freddy had found his 12 disciples. Those 12 sought and found 12 more and the process continued. As of April 1999, Freddy was responsible for more than 1,500 cell groups.

Freddy leads worship on Saturday night for over 18,000 young people. He meets weekly with César Fajardo, his discipler. He is a husband and father and has an active concert ministry throughout Latin America.

What is the secret of Freddy's success? From talking with Freddy over the years and observing his life, I've noticed at least three reasons for his success. First, Freddy is totally sold out to Jesus Christ. He understands clearly that only Christ can grant success. Freddy lives in close communion with Jesus and teaches his disciples that they must maintain intimacy with Jesus at all costs. Freddy expects his disciples to pray diligently, fast regularly and engage in spiritual warfare. God Himself has given Freddy a vision for multiplication and discipleship.

A second reason Freddy is so fruitful is because he believes in submission and authority. He submits to César Fajardo and meets with him each week. Like the centurion in the New Testament, Freddy Rodriguez is a "man under authority." With all of his multiple talents, Freddy could easily "make it on his own," but he chooses rather to submit himself to those over him. Because of Freddy's attitude, those under him are willing to submit to his authority.

Freddy's time commitment is a final reason for his success as a leader. Not only does he meet with his 12 each week, but he also meets with his entire discipleship network each week (the disciples of his disciples). In this way, Freddy has been able to maintain the quality control at the lower levels.

7

G-12 Principles

Your Church Can Use

People flock to ICM and see the model working like a well-tuned Corvette. They see the speed, the shiny paint and the leather seats. They look at the car and want one of their own. So they return home and try to put the model in place. They try to recreate the same car they saw in Colombia. Yet they forget to understand what is under the hood. Even when people look at the engine and hear it roar, they still don't understand how the engine works. So they buy the parts but don't know how to put it together. They miss the basic principles that lie beneath the beautiful exterior.

Anyone wanting to implement the G-12 model must discern the difference between function and form, principle and method. This is the way to apply the beneficial principles from ICM to your own church situation, thus preparing your church for growth.

CORE PRINCIPLES VERSUS
SUPPORTING PRINCIPLES

It's important to distinguish the essential principles from the supporting ones. The supporting principles can be found in other cell churches around the world and are not necessarily unique to ICM. The supporting principles are part of the overall mix of the church, but they don't form the foundation for the G-12 explosion. I recommend that you practice the core principles right now, whereas the supporting concepts might come later. The seven core principles are:

1. The G-12 model focuses on cell multiplication.
2. A cell group opens when a leader is trained.
3. Everyone who enters the church is a potential cell leader.
4. All believers are expected to enter cell leader training.
5. Every leader is a potential supervisor.
6. A person becomes a disciple when he or she opens a cell.
7. Everyone must be ministered to in order to minister.

CORE PRINCIPLE #1: THE G-12 MODEL FOCUSES ON CELL MULTIPLICATION

The G-12 model is primarily a multiplication model. It's a call to rapid and continuous multiplication of cell groups.[1]

César Castellanos implemented this model as a way to multiply his cell groups more rapidly. He endeavored to eliminate the obstacles of the traditional cell structure (e.g., geographical limitations, excess administration), so his church could grow exponentially. Since implementing this model, the church has grown from 70 cell groups to the present 20,000.

Pastor Castellanos never envisioned a closed form of intense discipleship disconnected from rapid church growth. I read about one church in transition to the G-12 model that touted its new emphasis of in-depth discipleship. This church even stated that with its new G-12 emphasis it was now concerned with spiritual growth rather than numerical growth.

Make no mistake about it; ICM is fervently concerned about numerical growth as well as spiritual growth. At ICM, if cell leaders don't multiply their groups they are set aside. Castellanos has a clear numerical goal, and the cell leaders diligently work to fulfill it. The G-12 model as practiced at ICM is more of a multiplication model than a discipleship model. It's a call to rapid and continuous multiplication of cell groups.

CORE PRINCIPLE #2: A CELL GROUP OPENS WHEN A LEADER IS TRAINED

In the common style of cell multiplication, the cell had to wait for a certain number of people and interns before the multiplication took place. Multiplication becomes a process of waiting for more people to attend the group — a focus on attendance instead of training new leadership. The problem with this model is that when the cell reaches the magical number "15" or "12" and the group is ready to multiply, some members quit, not wanting to experience the pain of separating from members of the group.

In the G-12 model, you can multiply your cell at any number: four, five, ten. The new leader does not depend upon the number attending the cell. Instead the new leader is sent off as a missionary from the parent group to plant his or her own cell. The new leader might take one or two from the parent cell, but he or she is encouraged to start the cell immediately. The new leader will maintain his relationship with the parent cell leader — now as a disciple. This makes cell multiplication easier and more efficient.

Tim Scheuer, church planter with the Church Army, writes about his G-12 transition: "Cells have more variety and possibilities on how groups start, who leads them and when they meet. Now groups can start wherever and however. Before we were bound by cell church legalism."[2]

CORE PRINCIPLE #3: EVERYONE WHO ENTERS THE CHURCH IS A POTENTIAL CELL LEADER

The story is told of Michelangelo passing by a huge chunk of marble that lay by the roadside. Another sculptor had become discouraged with the marble and discarded it. Michelangelo began to stare at that chunk of marble. He continued to stare until one of his friends became impatient and said, "What are you staring at?" Michelangelo looked up and said, "I'm staring at an angel." He could see something wonderful and worthwhile in a broken piece of stone.

The declared goal of ICM is to transform every new convert into a dynamic cell leader.[3] ICM seeks to convert each broken piece of clay into an angel. Perhaps this is the chief reason why ICM has experienced such amazing success. Pastor Castellanos counsels his cell leaders to envision each member of the cell as a future cell leader. No matter how set aside or broken down because of sin, Castellanos believes that God is all-powerful and able to make something beautiful of each person.

Some pastors and leaders believe that only those with the gift of evangelism or the gift of leadership are capable of leading a cell group. The goal is to discover "the gifted" in the congregation and then to train them to lead cell groups.

My statistical study of over 700 cell leaders supports the

convictions of Pastor Castellanos. My research revealed that the "anointing" to evangelize effectively and multiply a small group doesn't rest on a chosen few. The introverted, the uneducated and those in the lower social bracket were just as successful as their counterparts. Nor did one particular gift of the Spirit, such as evangelism, distinguish those who could multiply their groups from those who could not. Successful cell leaders don't solely depend on their own gifts. They rely on the Holy Spirit as they marshal the entire cell to reach family, friends and acquaintances.[4]

After having studied the G-12 model and noticing how each member is transformed into a cell leader, I encourage cell leaders to view all cell members as "potential cell leaders" and sponsor all of them to eventually become cell leaders. I've noticed that there are far too many "assistant cell leaders" who do nothing but occupy a title. Such a title draped over one or two people often hinders other members from assuming the role of cell leader. Harold Weitsz, pastor of Little Falls Christian Center in South Africa, echoes this thinking when he writes: "We do not speak of 'cell members' any longer, but of trainees to become cell leaders."[5]

Granted, not everyone will lead a group for a variety of reasons. But as soon as a small-group system is infected with the thinking that only certain people can lead a group, a great deal of broken marble will continue to dot the church landscape, forever classified as incapable.

CORE PRINCIPLE #4: ALL BELIEVERS ARE EXPECTED TO ENTER CELL LEADER TRAINING

Principle #3 (everyone a cell leader) and principle #4 (everyone entering an equipping track) are inseparable. When a church concludes that every cell member is a potential cell leader, the logical step is to train each person to eventually lead a cell group.

Castellanos often declares that he wants to prepare every member to lead and to bear fruit, not just to sit watching others do the ministry. He says, "Our goal is not to recruit cell members but to train leaders."[6] As soon as a new convert starts attending ICM, he or she is placed on the training path that ends in cell leadership. Involvement at ICM means entering the equipping track. If someone is a member at ICM and refuses to enter the training to become a cell leader, that person can always find another church that will allow him or her to attend the Sunday service and nothing more.

ICM's example is helping many churches to see the need of a clear equipping track in order to train each member for cell leadership. Tim Scheuer, church planter with the Church Army writes, "The change [to the G-12 model] motivated us to get our equipping track into place because now we see everyone as a leader."[7]

Core Principle #5: Every Leader Is a Potential Supervisor

If you understand this principle, you've grasped the heart of the G-12 model. This principle removes the shroud of mystery that so often obscures the G-12 model. Instead of the word "supervision," ICM uses the word "discipleship." You might use the word pastoring or shepherding. The idea is the same.

Simply put, the G-12 model asks each parent cell leader to supervise those new leaders who come from the parent cell. Supervisors are not appointed in the G-12 model. No one is waiting for a "calling" from above to become a supervisor.[8]

The beauty of the G-12 system is that it taps into the personal motivation of each individual leader. All energetic, entrepreneurial leaders can rise as high as their drive takes them. They can supervise (disciple) as many new leaders as their time and talents permit. The sky is the limit to those leaders who desire to achieve. No one is waiting for an appointment. You reap what you sow in the G-12 system.

For years at the Republic Church in Quito, Ecuador, we appointed supervisors to rotate among cell groups. After all, most cell churches did the same thing.

Now we give every cell leader the "green light" to become a supervisor. "Each of you is a supervisor," we tell them. "All you have to do is multiply your group, and you will supervise the new group(s) under your care."

Vinicio Reyes was appointed as supervisor under our previous cell system. Vinicio rotated among five groups. When we starting using G-12 principles, Vinicio was on the same playing field as everyone else. He had to prove himself, just like the others. Now he has to multiply his cell group. After multiplying his cell group, Vinicio naturally supervised (discipled) those daughter cell leaders that sprang from his own group. Currently, Vinicio is supervising two cell leaders with the goal of supervising five by the end of the year.

CORE PRINCIPLE #6: A PERSON BECOMES A DISCIPLE WHEN HE OR SHE OPENS A CELL

Every cell leader needs to help the members of the group through the training process, but in the end, a disciple is one of your 12 only when he or she has opened a cell group. This maintains the spotlight upon multiplication and not on an ingrown process of endless perfection.

CORE PRINCIPLE #7: EVERYONE MUST BE MINISTERED TO IN ORDER TO MINISTER

Principle #5 unveils the mystery behind the G-12 system, while principle #7 simplifies it. Often, people fall into the error of defining the G-12 system by a number of meetings. They adopt it or reject it on the basis of whether or not their church can add another meeting.

Such thinking fails to look beyond G-12 methodology to G-12 principles. The methodology is the number of meetings. The principle is that *everyone must be ministered to in order to minister*. Whether you require three meetings per week (ICM), two meetings per week (BWPC), 1.5 meetings per week (Republic Church)[9] or your own variation, you must minister to the ministers if they're going to continue to minister.

The number of meetings is not the issue. The key question is whether or not your cell leaders are receiving sufficient pastoral care and ministry. Determine what will accomplish the goal of caring for the cell leaders and put that system into place. Don't get stuck on the number of meetings.

OTHER SUPPORTING PRINCIPLES

Along with the core principles that I consider universals of the G-12 system, there are supporting principles that some have adopted from the G-12 model. The reason I consider them supporting principles is because they're not necessarily unique to ICM.

Leadership Training Must Be Given Chief Priority

This is a principle of ICM, but it's not solely unique to ICM. Most cell churches around the world emphasize this truth. Perhaps, ICM has made it more personal. Each cell leader, in other words, takes personal interest in guaranteeing that new converts pass through the leadership training. What is that personal interest? The desire to find 12 disciples. The earnest desire (and even natural competition) to have many disciples stirs each leader to develop as many potential leaders as possible.

Leadership Training Should Be Streamlined and Accelerated

The problem in many cell leadership training programs is that potential leaders get lost in the process. Perhaps there aren't enough options to train potential leaders. Perhaps, the leadership training course is so long that the would-be leader fizzles out because of other commitments.

At ICM, leadership training is effective because it's streamlined and achievable. Everyone knows the requirements and realizes that they can fulfill them.

Homogenous Cells Are Preferable To Geographical Cells

This is a fact at ICM but not a principle. ICM is leading the way because of its influence, but it's not the first cell church to emphasize homogenous cells. Faith Community Baptist Church (Singapore) has always based a large portion of its cells in homogenous groupings. At FCBC there are handicap cells, music ministry cells, young people's cells, etc.

We at the Republic Church have always organized our cells according to homogeneous divisions, rather than geographical boundaries. Thus, we never even recognized the homogeneous structure at ICM.

Obviously, the move away from strict geographical divisions revolutionized ICM.[10] This truth continues to have a powerful impact on other churches, and I think it's safe to say that the cell church worldwide is moving toward homogenous cells.

Any Successful Cell Leader Can Rise To Greater Positions

In the established Cho system, it seemed that you had to jump through more hoops to enter higher positions of leadership. With the G-12 system, the proof is in the pudding. If you multiply leaders who multiply leaders, the result will be many, many cell groups under your charge. In fact, the person who reaches 250 can obtain a part-time staff position at ICM. It is attainable and everyone starts on the same level.

In the Cho system, there isn't as much motivation once you reached the heights of say, a district pastor. In the G-12 system, the counting never ceases. For example, you will always know how many cell groups Freddy Rodriguez or Luis Salas has, even when that number is over 2,000.

Your Co-leaders Become Your Assistants

César says that every one of his 12 could take his place if he were to leave the church. After the attempted assassination, pastor Castellanos was forced to remain in Houston, Texas for seven months. One of his assistants began leading the church. When César left there were 10,700 cell groups, and when he returned there were some 17,000 cell groups. Even without him, the number of cells exploded. The success of ICM doesn't hinge on one person.

Castellanos counsels others, "When you go to preach somewhere, leave one of your 12 in charge of the work."[11] Top leadership at ICM emphasizes the importance of delegating their ministry, since the goal is to develop a team of 12. ICM realizes that in order to grow, it must continually develop new leadership.

GET YOUR ENGINE RUNNING RIGHT

Just as the motor makes a beautiful Corvette run, the principles make ICM's G-12 model hum. The good news is that you don't need to go to Bogota to use them. Apply the above principles to your own unique situation, and you'll increase the effectiveness of your ministry.

8

BLAZING

NEW TRAILS

In 1792, an unknown English pastor, part-time teacher and shoemaker began a revolution. His name was William Carey. He refused to accept the teaching in his day that the Great Commission was no longer relevant for the church. When he had the opportunity to address a group of ministers, he challenged them to give a reason why the Great Commission did not apply to them. They rebuked him, saying, "When God chooses to win the heathen, He will do it without your help or ours." Yet Carey believed in his vision so strongly he became part of it and sailed as a missionary to India, thus launching the modern missionary movement.

Few possess the boldness to launch out into the deep, leaving behind conventional wisdom in order to blaze new trails. Most people prefer to follow the status quo — the tried-and true.

In *The Leadership Challenge*, authors James Kouzes and Barry Posner say, "Leaders venture out. Those who lead others to greatness seek and accept challenge. Leaders are pioneers — people who are willing to step out into the unknown. They're willing to take risks, to innovate and experiment in order to find new and better ways of doing things."[1]

David Yonggi Cho and César Castellanos are both innovative pioneers. Both blazed trails that the worldwide cell church is now following. Like Carey, these church leaders refused to accept the status quo and followed their own convictions. The purpose of this chapter is to help you blaze your own trail — to adapt the principles that work best for you. In chapters ten and 11, you'll read about how 12 churches have applied the principles of the G-12 model to their own context. In this chapter, you'll understand the strengths and weaknesses of both the 5x5 model (Cho) and the G-12 model (Castellanos). After comparing the tracks these two men of God laid down, my counsel is that you steal the best and apply the principles that work for you.

SIMILARITIES OF THE TWO MODELS

The path ICM forged is not entirely new. There are many similarities, in fact, between the G-12 system at ICM and the 5x5 model. Both models, for example, are similar in purpose — to provide support, care and leadership for cell leaders. In both systems, the cell group is the same. The cells use the same order, focus on discipleship and evangelism, and are based on the senior pastor's teaching.[2] Both models view cell ministry as the backbone of the church, the primary way to pastor the congregation, raise up new leadership and evangelize non-Christians. The goal in both cell systems is to integrate cell members into the life of the local church.

Distinctions between the Two Models

In other ways, the 5x5 model and the G-12 model are different. The 5x5 model is more *hierarchical and top-heavy*. Positions and titles are clear and distinct, and the entire system is easier to understand and control. Under this system, a supervisor cares for five cell leaders; a zone pastor directs 25 cell leaders; and a district pastor supervises approximately 125 cell leaders. A zone averages about 250 people in 25 cells, and a district numbers about 1,250 people in 125 cells. (This exact numbering of 5x5 is not strictly followed in every cell model.)[3]

Even the offices in the 5x5 structure clearly delineate the different positions and geographical territories for each district, zone and sector of the city. Clarity, control, and leadership hierarchy characterize the 5x5 system. The structure looks something like this:

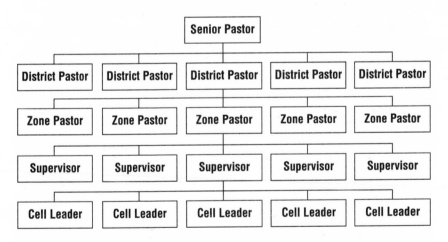

In the 5x5 model, there is a necessity for a fairly large staff of paid workers at the church. When someone is paid full-time to do the work of ministry, it frees him or her to accomplish more than would be possible in a voluntary role, but it also changes the nature of the relationship between the paid-staff member and the one receiving the supervision.

The G-12 structure, on the other hand, is a *grass-roots system.* Like the complex underground root system of a giant oak tree, the G-12 administration functions below the surface. There are very few titles in this structure. The staff pastors who also lead the homogeneous departments are the only paid positions. The rest of the workers are volunteers. The G-12 structure looks like this when mapped out:

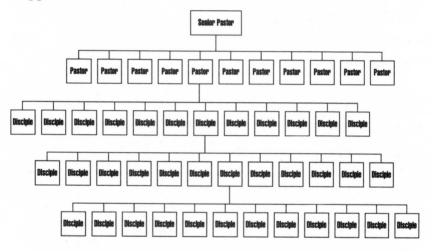

A more dynamic representation resembles this:

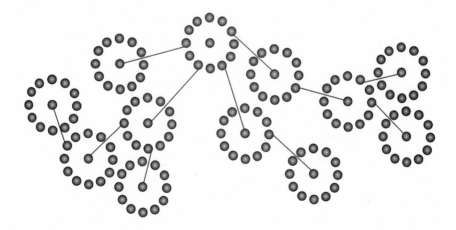

In the 5x5 model, oversight takes place predominately by individuals who have served as cell leaders, but have been *removed from active cell involvement* into more of a supervisory role. Although they continue to attend cells, they do so in a different capacity.

They are there primarily to observe, to critique, to encourage and to exhort. Because they move from cell to cell, it is difficult for them to maintain deep intimate relationships within the cell or to participate actively in the cell.

In the G-12 model, the majority of workers *continue to lead* a cell, while pastoring/discipling other cell leaders. Regardless of their stature or position in the church, they continue to have the weekly experience of participating in a cell.

In the G-12 model, *cell groups multiply across the entire city*. They are limited by homogeneity as opposed to geography. In a pure 5x5 structure, even the *multiplication of cell groups must occur within geographical confines*. (The 5x5 model allows for homogeneity within the geographical boundaries.) If a cell in District 3, Zone 1, sector 4 multiplies into Zone 2, sector 3, that cell comes under the leadership of another zone pastor and supervisor. This is not the case in the G-12 model. Youth cells, men's cells and women's cells can multiply across the entire city.[4]

STRENGTHS OF THE 5x5 MODEL

More Quality Control

The 5x5 structure continues to add higher level leadership as the cell system grows. For every five units (cells, sectors, zones, districts) new higher-level leadership is added. This helps maintain the quality control.[5]

Healthier Cell Groups
Cell groups in the 5x5 model are often more healthy. Two factors make this possible: First, there is a higher ratio of supervision: one supervisor per five cells instead of one discipler per 12 cells. Second, cell groups start with a fixed number of people. The emphasis is on mother-daughter multiplication, rather than cell planting. Thus, when the cell starts, there is already a group consciousness. In the G-12 model this group consciousness often doesn't occur right away.

Easily Understood
This model has been around longer and is more easily understood. With its emphasis on positions, titles and specific geographical delineation, most people immediately understand it. Part of the reason for the clarity is the ability to map each aspect of the system. In 5x5 churches, huge district offices mark the location of all workers. At a glance, you can recognize this system.

More Success in Tracking Progress
In the 5x5 model, it is possible to maintain up-to-date records of all activities. Since this system maintains higher levels of leadership as the system expands, these leaders can devote more time to compiling and analyzing the data. This information allows the staff to better understand the situation and make corrections according to the needs.

WEAKNESSES OF THE 5X5 MODEL

Particular Members Are Commissioned to Lead Cell Groups
Generally, the 5x5 model chooses certain gifted members as leaders over others. The concept of "every member a leader" is not practiced. Again, the emphasis on titles (supervisor, leader, assistant leader, host, etc.) separates leaders from non-leaders. Talented and gifted people

enter the training to become leaders, and this type of selection continues to higher levels of leadership in the hierarchical leadership structure.

Too Much Hierarchy

The danger in the 5x5 model is the inactivity of middle managers (supervisor, zone pastor, district pastor). Often, those in such positions lose touch with the life of the cell because they concentrate on supervising cell leaders instead of actively being involved in the ministry. Larry Stockstill's insight is helpful:

> North America has moved away from middle management. Some cell structures emphasize this middle management and set up a corporate type structure (district pastor, zone pastors, etc.). The three levels are just supervising and not winning souls. All levels should be winning souls. No one should just sit back and do nothing. Everyone in the church should be winning souls. Everybody.[6]

Break-up of Relationships

In the 5x5 model, the cell multiplication process causes breaks in relationships. Close bonds within cell groups are severed when the group multiplies. The new cell comes under the jurisdiction of the area supervisor, not the original cell leader.

Multiplication within Geographical Boundaries

In the 5x5 geographical model, if a group is ready to give birth and the new leader lives in a different zone, he or she would be forced to come under the supervision of another zone leader, thus separating ties with the parent group. Because of this separation, the parent cell leader loses contact with that new cell.

Cell members are restricted to winning neighbors and contacts that live in the same geographical area. Yet, friendships in today's fast-changing society are often developed in the workplace, university, or a restaurant. Neighbour says, "The difficulty with a geographical structure is that people often have no natural contact with their neighbors and eventually run out of *oikos* contacts (friendship circle) that can be reached."[7]

STRENGTHS OF THE G-12 MODEL

Every Person Is a Leader
The G-12 system is designed to develop leaders. It takes the commitment to the belief in the priesthood of all believers to a new level. The equipping is designed to prepare everyone for leadership and no one is allowed to stand by and watch.

Relationships Are Maintained
Because the leader who multiplies his or her cell supervises the new group, relationships between cell groups are maintained. In this system, multiplication without division occurs. The parent cell leader maintains close relationships with the new cell leader and even invites him or her back to the parent cell. Since there are no geographical hindrances in the G-12 model, cells can multiply throughout the city without coming under the supervision of another leader.

Less Hierarchy
This model requires less hierarchy and can be implemented on a grass-roots level. There is greater potential for exponential growth in the G-12 model because less outward structure is needed to make it work. Each leader can become a supervisor. Leaders don't have to be

promoted to occupy an official leadership position. All leaders can rise to the height of their talent and success.

More Adaptable

The G-12 model is a fluid model that can connect to any type of structure. For example, if you choose to organize your cells according to geography, you could still use the G-12 system. If you choose to organize the cells according to homogeneous groupings or ministry department, the G-12 works just fine. A key strength is its adaptability. This is not true of the 5x5 model in which the leadership positions are even named according to the geographical divisions (zone servant, district pastor, etc.).

Less Staff Required

Some point out that the G-12 model requires less staff. ICM, for example, doesn't hire a full-time pastor until he or she has 500 cell groups. The G-12 model lends itself to more of a grass roots care structure, thus reducing the need for salaried personnel. It's true, however, that even in the 5x5 structure you don't necessarily need to pay higher level leadership. The Love Alive Church in Tegucigalpa, Honduras, which has 1,000 cells in the 5x5 structure, expects voluntary service from all zone pastors. The church did not provide financial support for its four district pastors until 1996.

Multiplication Occurs More Rapidly

Multiplication occurs more rapidly and greater potential exists for continual multiplication of cell groups (some have over 1,000). There are no boundaries to multiplication in the G-12 model.

WEAKNESSES OF THE G-12 MODEL

Greater Time Commitment

The G-12 model requires a greater time commitment. Parent cell leaders are asked to supervise those who start new groups, thus increasing the time commitment. The ICM G-12 system requires three meetings per week. This is a great drawback for many — especially in North America. Mike Atkins, former senior pastor of the Church of the Nations, writes:

> This difficult challenge seems to be in convincing individuals who have never experienced cell life that they will find it rewarding enough to be willing to invest two periods of time a week to active and personal participation. Unquestionably, there will be those whose lifestyles or priorities simply will not allow them to make this level of time commitment. For others, it will merely be a matter of allowing them to experience cells; the joy and rewarding experience will sell itself when it comes to asking them to make the commitment to lead a cell as well.[8]

Quality Control

The organizational chart in the G-12 system flows downward and new levels of leadership are not added to sustain quality control. The quality control can therefore falter as cell groups multiply at lower levels. In contrast, the 5x5 model constantly adds higher level leadership as the organizational system expands. One of Castellanos' 12, Rafael Perez, admits that degeneration takes place within the G-12 model. The original 12 understand the vision. The farther away a disciple is from the original discipler, the more the purity of the vision falters.

To further this problem, some G-12 churches lack clear, consistent statistical reporting.[9] Because the cells that multiply far below escape the attention of the pastoral staff, it's difficult to get clear, up-to-date data on what's happening at lower levels.

Weaker Cell Groups

Since the G-12 system asks each cell member to start a cell group (often from scratch), cells tend to start with only one or two people. Thus, it takes longer for a cell to develop a group consciousness. Some of these cell plants never arrive at this group level and fizzle out or cease.

Permanency of the Disciple

The G-12 model also asks each person to find 12 permanent disciples. Some might hesitate to commit to a permanent discipleship group. Why? Because of the desire for personal freedom and not wanting to come under the control of someone else in a discipleship relationship.[10]

CHOOSING AMONG THE ALTERNATIVES

Hindsight is clearer than foresight. The trails that David Yonggi Cho and César Castellanos blazed for the church make it easier for us to see the road ahead. Yet, you don't have to commit your church to the 5x5 model or the G-12 model. I recommend, in fact, that you base your transition on principles, rather than outward structures. Take the best of both worlds and then blaze your own trail.

WARNING:

G-12 LANDMINES

In 1991, sculptor-painter John Buckley visited Cambodia. After gaining interest in its turbulent history, he traveled to Phnom Penh, the capital city, to witness the effects of 25 years of war on a nation struggling to rebuild itself. Traveling initially to do a series of drawings, he instead became involved in the city's hospitals, taking casts and fitting artificial limbs to landmine victims. He writes, "The sun on my back, blue skies, lush tropical plants, the rusty soil, the waves of light across the paddy fields, the jungle . . . it was all memorable. And yet I was transfixed. I came away with one feeling, one image — the agony of the limbless from the landmines."[1]

Landmines are one of the most horrible inventions of modern war. They still pose an awful risk in Cambodia and preventative measures must be taken. This chapter will help you avoid the pitfalls and landmines that could derail your G-12 experiment.

LANDMINE #1: ADOPTING THE G-12 BEFORE ESTABLISHING CELL CHURCH VALUES

This landmine is subtle. You won't see it because it touches the invisible realm of values in the cell church. If you adopt the G-12 model before establishing cell church values, you'll be disappointed when your cells falter. You might even blame the G-12 model for your failure.

What are those biblical values important in cell church ministry? One of them is the value of the priesthood of all believers. This truth opens the door of possibilities for every person in your church. Each person has great worth and has the potential to lead a cell and pastor the flock. César Castellanos says:

> The growth of our church has come from our cell ministry. Between 500 and 1,000 people are converted each Sunday. It would be impossible to pastor them if it were not for the cell ministry. In the cell group, the leader acts as the pastor who teaches, counsels and answers the questions of the new believers.[2]

If a church is closed to the concept of every-member ministry and believes that it must depend on *the* pastor to care for the members, implementing the G-12 system will not produce the desired growth. You must first implement the value that every member of the church is a minister.

The commitment to community is another important value in the cell church. If you simply add the G-12 model over a program-oriented church, you will encounter problems. Again, Castellanos says:

The cell group [system] is not one program in the church. [It is] the program. Everything that is done must be based on cell ministry. The cells make our church a living congregation and enable us to penetrate every social status. In every corner of the city there is a cell group from ICM that meets at least once per week. These groups meet in houses, offices, etc.[3]

You must first make your cells the basic community in your church. You must protect your cells from the myriad of programs that will compete with them. After these values are firmly established in your church, the G-12 model will help you strengthen and fine-tune your cell church.

Another cell church value is the commitment to evangelize through the multiplication of cell groups. If your church, for example, lacks a commitment to evangelism and multiplication of cell groups, adding the G-12 model won't suddenly make your church more outreach oriented.

LANDMINE #2: PRIORITIZING G-12 GROUPS OVER CELL GROUPS

The G-12 structure helps *cell groups* stay healthy. The G-12 structure is like the scaffolding at a building site. The scaffolding supports the workers who are constructing the building. But the focus is always the building and not the scaffolding. The focus in the G-12 model must always be the cell.

The G-12 system must never be allowed to develop a life of its own and compete with the cell. Your church *should not* be known as a G-12 church. It should be recognized as a cell church.

You should avoid anything that competes with the cell focus — including the G-12 model. I know of some churches that promote bimonthly cell meetings in order to have bimonthly G-12 meetings. This might save time, but you'd be tampering with the life of the cell. Ralph Neighbour says, "As far as I am concerned the G-12 is a management structure and in no way replaces the cell as the basic Christian community!"[4] Your cell groups must always be your focus; *the G-12 system is a way to care for your cell leaders, not a system that runs parallel to the cells and thus competes with them.*

I know of another cell church that counts their G-12 meetings as cell groups. When they announce the total number of cell groups in the church, they include the G-12 groups. I would advise you not to do this. A G-12 group is not a cell group. The G-12 group is a pastoral care/discipleship group for cell leaders, but it's not the cell. The cell must always be the foundation of your church.

LANDMINE #3: CONTROLLING OTHERS

The shepherding movement flourished in the 70's. It placed shepherds over small groups to care for the sheep. This movement sought to correct the lack of discipleship in the church. The right focus of care and discipleship soon degenerated into the wrong motivation of power and control. Forced subjection replaced personal liberty, and many people fell headlong into bondage.

Don't fall into the trap of trying to control the sheep. Don't place anyone under your bondage or your discipleship.

"Disciple" in ancient literature means pupil or learner. The Greek noun "disciple" is derived from the Greek verb which means "to learn." In the Greek world, philosophers were surrounded by their pupils. The Jews claimed to be disciples of Moses (John 9:28); the followers of John the Baptist were known as his disciples (Mark 2:18; John 1:35). The word "disciple" came to signify the adherent of a particular outlook in religion or philosophy.

Jesus had his disciples (followers) as well. Sometimes this word refers to those who responded to His message (Matt. 5:1; Luke 6:17; 19:37), while at other times it referred more narrowly to those who accompanied him on his travels (Mark 6:45; Luke 8:2f.; 10:1), and especially to the 12 apostles (Mark 3:14). Jesus taught his 12 by spending time with them and practically instructing them as they reflected on personal experience. He sent his disciples to do the work of ministry — preaching the gospel, casting out demons and healing the sick (Mark 3:14f.).[5]

The word "disciple" is used 240 times in the gospels and 30 times in Acts, but never is it used in the epistles. Even in the book of Acts the overriding use of the word "disciple" is descriptive for the followers of Jesus, not for the followers of someone else.

Never is the word "disciple" used to promote personal discipleship. The Scripture stands against believers advancing their own agenda by "making disciples." Paul warned the believers at Corinth: "One of you says, 'I follow Paul'; another, 'I follow Apollos'; another, 'I follow Cephas'; still another, 'I follow Christ.' Is Christ divided? Was Paul crucified for you? Were you baptized into the name of Paul?" (1 Cor. 1:12-13). Paul warns again in Acts 20:30-31: "Even from your own number men will arise and distort the truth in order to draw away disciples after them. So be on your guard! Remember that for three years I never stopped warning each of you night and day with tears."

You should have a godly hesitancy about calling believers "your disciples."[6] We are called to make followers of Jesus Christ. The true mark of a disciple is the image of Christ. The shepherding movement in North America went astray by promoting an unhealthy dependence between disciple and leader. Your goal as a discipler is to create in your disciple a dependence on Jesus Christ, not on yourself.

Perhaps to protect the church against this error, the Holy Spirit inspired the New Testament writers to use the words believers, saints and brothers to describe followers of Jesus. In Acts 11:26 we read: "The disciples were called Christians first at Antioch." After Acts chapter 21 the word "disciple" no longer appears.

The church of Jesus Christ as the Body of Christ and the temple of the Holy Spirit was born on the day of Pentecost. From then on, the making of disciples was different. The maturing and equipping of Christians happens in the body of Christ and in the temple of God as manifested in local congregations.

The G-12 model is a great way to organize your church in order to supervise and pastor every leader. Yet, great care should be taken to avoid name-calling: "John is the disciple of Scott," "Mary is Joan's disciple," and so forth. There's no need to distinguish ourselves by saying, "I'm in the 12 of so-and-so."

ICM promotes the discipleship relationship lasting permanently. They don't see it as a two or three year commitment. Rather, they view each G-12 group as a relationship between parents and children. It lasts a lifetime.[7] The idea of permanency is a two-edged sword. On the positive side, a long-term commitment can be a great blessing. On the negative side, it might negate the person's freedom of choice. A disciple should never feel bondage or heaviness in a G-12 group, nor should he or she feel under compulsion to remain in the same discipleship relationship permanently.

LANDMINE #4: CHOOSING ONE DISCIPLE OVER ANOTHER

I've heard people say, "When you're looking for those to form part of your G-12 group, choose the best and the brightest." This idea of selecting one person over another can be a dangerous, deadly landmine. If you're leading a cell group and one of your members opens a new cell group, shouldn't that person automatically form part of your G-12 group? The answer is a resounding *yes*.[8]

It's dangerous to say: "Well, I don't really like that person, so I'll let someone else take him or her." Such an attitude will surely lead toward divisiveness.

Or perhaps one leader decides to tack-on extra requirements, like spending two hours in daily devotions, meeting one on one with every disciple or fasting two days per week.

Then what happens to those who open cell groups under that person, but can't quite fulfill all the requirements? Who will care for these leaders? I've often heard this answer: "I'll just give such a person to one of my disciples." This sounds easy, but the person who just can't measure-up will invariably feel like a loser. Such thinking creates a competitive mentality.

Rather, the person who opens a new cell is discipled by the parent cell leader. The G-12 model is an effective way to care for cell leaders and a way to multiply cells. Don't allow it to separate the super-spiritual from the rest.

If you're transitioning your cell church to the G-12 model and you have several pastors on staff, the senior pastor should pick his staff members as part of his G-12. Regardless of your pastoral care structure, in the cell church the senior pastor always oversees his top cell pastors. It's not as if the senior pastor can say, "I think I'll pick Pastor Tom as one of my 12 but not Pastor Dick." Imagine the rift this could cause!

This is true of cell leaders as well. Suppose you want to transition your church to the G-12 model and you already have a number of cells functioning. It's not wise to allow top leadership to pick-and-choose based on personal preference.

I suggest, rather, that during the transition time, existing cell leaders should be placed under G-12 leaders. For example, suppose

John is a zone pastor who has five supervisors under him. Those five supervisors should be the first five of John's 12. One of those supervisors under John is Mark. Mark has five small groups under his care. Those five small group leaders would form Mark's first five disciples.

After making those initial decisions based on the cells that already exist, each cell leader would choose his or her disciples based on those who start new cells from the parent cell.

LANDMINE #5: DEMANDING TOO MANY MEETINGS

In order to sell the G-12 system to your church, you'll need to understand this landmine and how to avoid it. You might ruin your chances of even implementing the G-12 structure in your church if you decree a time commitment that your people can't handle.

You should not equate the G-12 system with simply adding more meetings.

Granted, adding more meetings to most endeavors in life will produce better results. Suppose that I'm teaching a semester class that meets once per week. Suddenly I tell my students that the class will now meet three times per week for the same time period. Do you think the students will learn more? No doubt. But they will also have to juggle other commitments — including family.

Adding more time to something usually (not always) produces results, but we live in a world full of commitments. You must respect those commitments in your followers. Again, if the G-12 model is primarily a time-intensive model, there is reason to question its validity. You could probably add extra meetings to your present small group system and discover amazing results. Probably the reason that you haven't added additional time commitments is because you respect the present time commitments of your people.

Effective cell leaders already must spend quality time developing new relationships — the friendship dinner with the neighbors, the Neighborhood Watch meeting, playing sports with a work associate. And then there are the leadership training commitments that will assure future leadership in your groups. Too many heavy discipleship requirements might deter future leaders from their main goal: cell leadership and reproduction.

To reduce the G-12 concept to more meetings is to miss the principles behind this system. In chapter seven, I focused on G-12 principles, one of which was the need to minister to the ministers. The meeting is merely the place where the ministry occurs.

After returning from a visit to ICM, two of our staff pastors insisted on following ICM's practice of requiring three meetings per week. The leaders under me, however, already had a plethora of commitments. My leaders were full-time professionals, who are mature, self-starters. They didn't need two more group meetings.

I couldn't demand such a time commitment. Many of you reading this book are pastors. You're full-time in the ministry. But your lay people are not. They have full-time jobs; they have additional weeknight commitments; they must care for their families, and they must lead their own open cell group.

On the other hand, it is important for a church to *determine the minimum time commitment* for a G-12 group to meet. Flexibility is great, but it does have its limits. If G-12 meetings are too infrequent, it's doubtful that effective pastoring and discipleship will occur.

ICM has determined that every G-12 leader should meet three times per week until he or she has found his 144. At that point, they only have two meetings per week.

Bethany World Prayer Center asks the new leaders to return to the parent cell group each week. This cuts the meeting load time down to two meetings per week. In that sense, it's very positive. Yet, the weakness of this approach is that it's hard for in-depth care and supervision to take place in an open cell group. In other words, does the new cell leader really need to return to an open cell group each week? Will an open cell group meet the needs of a new cell leader? Maybe at first, but I've discovered that after a few months, the new cell leader doesn't really need to come back to the parent cell. He or she is content in the new cell group.

At the Republic Church, we as the pastoral team decided that a G-12 group must meet at least once per month. For example, I have seven disciples at this time. I must meet with those seven as a group at least once per month. They in turn must meet with their disciples at least once per month. This means that two additional meetings occur each month for parent cell leaders (G-12 leaders).

Now that doesn't mean that I don't contact my disciples on a personal basis or that my disciples don't meet personally with their disciples. Normally once per month I have a personal meeting with each of them, and I often contact them by telephone.

You might do it differently. It's important that you find the right balance for you and that you *focus on meeting needs.* Effective leadership means taking into account the needs of the followers. It's important to ask your followers: "How can I best meet your needs?"

Understandably, new disciples don't really know what they need, but even with new disciples, you must respect their time and their commitments. Don't assume that they can meet each week with you. If they can, go for it. But be ready for a bimonthly meeting or even a monthly meeting.

Remember that the G-12 system is a support system. It's a care system much like the Jethro model. G-12 is not synonymous with another weekly meeting. It does mean that the needs of the disciples are met.

LANDMINE #6: INSISTING ON THE NUMBER 12

This is a landmine only if you insist on the number 12. Some leaders might reject the entire G-12 care system if they're forced to settle for the number 12. Is there biblical evidence for the number 12? Yes, some. God chose 12 tribes of Israel and Christ handpicked 12 disciples. Other arguments for the number 12 include the 12 months of the Hebrew calendar, the 12-hour day, and that 12 is often linked with the elective purposes of God.[9]

But other numbers have important significance in the Bible: six, seven, 40 and 70, to name a few. I see, in fact, very little evidence in the New Testament that the apostles specifically looked for 12 disciples. You won't find this process recorded in the book of Acts. Nor is the number 12 mentioned in the epistles. It's doubtful, therefore, that Christ intended the number 12 to become normative for His Church.

While you should avoid any fixation on the number 12, realize that a specific number gives each leader a target. It helps a person to expect more and better results. Whether that number is 12 or seven, a particular number aids each leader to envision multiplying his or her cell more than once. With such a goal, the leader won't be content with only one or two. The psychology is: "I must have my 12." Larry Stockstill concurs: "A certain boredom sets into cell leaders who have multiplied their groups. They lose motivation. But if you tell a cell leader that their life-time goal is to open 12 groups who will then open 12 groups, [there is continual motivation]."[10]

For example, before implementing the G-12 system at the Republic Church, we told our cell leaders that they would supervise the daughter cells that they multiplied. Yet, many of our leaders were content with multiplying and supervising just one or two cells. Then we gave each person the goal of supervising 12 cells, and our leaders could not rest content with supervising just one or two.

I think it's unwise to set a larger number than 12. Trying to minister to more than 12 leaders in a group situation is difficult because of the lack of intimacy (the higher the number the less intimacy). Could you reduce the number to ten or even five? Yes, I believe so.

LANDMINE #7: INSISTING ON STRICT HOMOGENEOUS CATEGORIES

ICM fell into this landmine in 1998. They began to insist on rigid homogeneity. If John was in the men's department, he could only disciple other men in a G-12 group. In 1998, ICM went one step further and said that John's open cell group must also be exclusively male. This created a forced, limiting situation in which only one gender could attend the open cell. I was glad to hear that in 1999 ICM changed this requirement and once again gave the open cell groups more liberty.

ICM continues to teach that men must disciple other men under the homogeneous discipleship network called "men." If you want to disciple others as a couple, you must be under another network called "couples."

I feel that such rigidity is unnecessary. As you transition to the G-12 model, you don't need to use such tight categories. My advice is that you allow the cells to multiply naturally and that each cell leader cares and disciples whomever opens a group under his or her leadership.

LANDMINE #8: TRYING TO FIX SOMETHING THAT'S NOT BROKEN

New church growth fads and methods abound. Don't implement the G-12 model just because others are doing it. If you're experiencing success in your cell ministry, don't try to change it. Jay Firebaugh, pastor at East Side Grace Brethren Church in Columbus, OH, prefers the 5x5 structure. He writes:

> Some people get excited about the G-12 model because they won't have to tear their relationships through multiplying their cell. However, it has been our experience that cells must regularly add new life or they'll dry up. This isn't to say that the G-12 model isn't working. But in our context, we found the 5x5 model to work better! Further, we've found evangelism to work best when the very people for whom you are "team fishing" are reached by the cell you are a part of and then ultimately come right into your cell to be equipped and discipled by the very people who worked together to reach them.[11]

Don't tell those at Elim Church that they need to change to the G-12 model. With 110,000 people attending their 5,500 cell groups, they're doing something right! Is your cell system working for you? You might not feel the need to change. If it's not broken, don't fix it.

10

G-12 PRINCIPLES FROM
NORTH AMERICAN CHURCHES

We've all heard the statement: "It may work in other countries, but it won't work here." Maybe deep inside you've been wondering how something in Bogota applies to North America. Jeannette Buller, a well-known teacher in U.S. cell church circles, pinpointed this concern when she said, "In an ideal world, I think the groups of 12 are the way to go. I'm still wrestling with how it will be contextualized to the U.S."[1]

I see two options with the G-12 model: First, apply the entire model. Second, apply the key principles only. You'll notice in this chapter that most churches have followed the church growth axiom — *Don't follow methods, rather extract the underlying principles from the methods and apply them to your situation.*[2]

CHURCH ARMY

BRANSON, MO • CHURCH PLANTER TIM SCHEUER

FACTS: NINE CELL GROUPS[3]

Tim Scheuer is an example of a leader who adapted the G-12 model to fit his own unique circumstances. Tim first adopted the cell strategy as the best way to reach people, and then began applying the G-12 model to fine-tune his system.

Tim's church is unusual. Take its mission statement: *Our target is the least, the last and the lost.* This church pursues the drug addict, the homeless and the outcast. Those who attend the church come from the "fringe," the dregs of society. Tim writes, "We are privileged to work with the folks that are close to the heart of Jesus."[4]

Pastor Tim has chosen to apply principles rather than adopt the entire G-12 model. He discovered, for example, that not all of the cell leaders were able to participate in two cell meetings a week. Time and distance simply didn't allow his people to attend two weekly meetings.

About this, Tim writes, "What we have tried to do is to separate the 'principle' from the 'method.' The principle being that everyone is ministered to and then ministers, the method being that you come to two cell groups each week." Tim discovered that for many in his church, the method of two meetings was simply not possible. He still encourages everyone to attend two groups, but there's also a great deal of flexibility.

Because Pastor Tim's church exists to reach sin-caked sinners for Jesus Christ, one of his chief attractions to the Bogota model centers on the Encounter weekends.

When he first heard about the Encounter events, he copied the entire Bogota Encounter weekend. Yet, Pastor Tim isn't afraid to test, prove and make adjustments. They changed their Encounter philosophy when they realized that they were focusing too much on the leader as the person with the "powerful anointing." Tim writes: "We were not satisfied with our ability to do the ministry."[5]

For this reason, the church turned to Neil Anderson's training on resolving personal and spiritual conflicts, which they felt was better suited to meet their needs. The Anderson approach placed the emphasis on the individual's receiving the ministry to embrace the responsibility for applying the truth that sets him or her free. Tim writes:

> The thought that strikes me is that if I needed a "powerfully anointed" minister to help me find freedom, when the enemy attacks me I will tend to assume I need to go and receive ministry from a person again. If I received my freedom through a process that I was responsible for, then when the enemy attacks I have learned through that process that "I" have authority "In Christ" over the attack of the enemy.

Since implementing G-12 principles, the church has gained momentum and expectancy. The G-12 strategy has helped free them from a "cell church legalism" and now everyone is ministered to and then ministers. Tim writes, "Now people are thinking constantly about starting new groups."[6]

FAITH COMMUNITY CHURCH
FOURSQUARE GOSPEL CHURCH OF CANADA
HALIFAX, NOVA SCOTIA, CANADA • PASTOR REID STAIRS
FACTS: 14 CELLS; 90 SUNDAY ATTENDANCE

The G-12 model has injected new flexibility and creativity into this congregation and corrected two areas of weakness found in its previous pastoral system:

1. The pain of releasing relationships every time groups multiplied.
2. The removal of the very best and most effective cell leaders out of active "cell" ministry to become zone supervisors.

In the previous 5x5 system, they felt like they were serving the model rather than the model serving them. Pastor Reid heard about the G-12 model in February 1998 and immediately shared the concept with his church leadership.

In May 1998, the church began to restructure. Reid and his wife chose 12 "disciples," and from those original leaders, several were selected to build groups from the remaining members of the congregation.

By using the G-12 system, the church discovered more ways to multiply cell groups. They could plant cells as well as give birth to fully functioning daughter cells. For example, one of the ladies was caring for two terminally ill senior adults one evening a week. With the new G-12 strategy in mind, she began to see her meeting as a potential cell. She led the wife to faith in Christ, and then she invited others to join them in the home for worship, prayer and ministry. Under the old system they would have never thought of this group as a "cell."

The G-12 model has also helped the church understand the priesthood of all believers. Now, everyone is a disciple of Christ. By focusing on Matt. 28:19, the church has come to believe that everyone has one basic calling — to be a disciple (which includes the commission to disciple).

They no longer focus on identifying potential cell leaders, since they assume that everyone will eventually lead others. For this reason, they now promote a more natural supervisory structure and a simplified equipping track. FCC no longer uses several tracks in their equipping system (i.e., one for disciple, cell leader, supervisor, pastor, etc.). Now it uses one track, which prepares everyone to lead a cell and then supervise those new leaders who start new cells. G-12 principles have helped Faith Community Church become more relevant to their own context and culture.

NEWMARKET ALLIANCE CHURCH
ONTARIO, CANADA • PASTOR DAVID BRANDON
FACTS: 40 CELLS; 350 SUNDAY ATTENDANCE

"Finally, freedom!" a participant cried out during the retreat. Freedom sums up the atmosphere at Newmarket as a result of the G-12 strategy. Pastor David says, "Somehow the previous ways of doing cells was not flexible enough to allow creativity in how groups were started and how people became leaders. Now there is incredible increase in possibilities."

Pastor Brandon reacted negatively when he first heard about the G-12 philosophy. He liked the tight, easily understood 5x5 structure. The free-flowing G-12 strategy seemed so messy to him.

Yet, after seven years, the entire leadership acknowledged that the 5x5 cell model was not working for them. Since the 5x5 model failed to meet their expectations, the leadership team encouraged Pastor Brandon to run with the G-12 philosophy. Pastor Brandon guided the church to make the change, and in one year all of the cells had incorporated themselves into the G-12 system.

The G-12 philosophy gave them a new freedom and power to multiply cell groups. Pastor Brandon writes:

The G-12 model has solved a problem we could not lick with the old 5x5, namely the reluctance of people to multiply their cell. Today I understand why. We were violating the innate desire people have to stay in a deep intimate relationship where they are comforted, strengthened, encouraged and even admonished while at the same time, building the kingdom. It is not that people do not want to multiply cells — they do not want to do it at the cost of losing the "one anothers" of Scripture that only mature in a long-term, loving relationship.

Cell multiplication is now a creative experience. When someone at NWAC starts meeting with even one other person, they consider this group to be a new cell and encourage them to bring others into their fellowship. Thus groups are easily started and can quickly grow. Newmarket Alliance defines a cell group as " . . . at least two people and no more than 12 who regularly meet for the purpose of nurturing discipleship through mutual Biblical edification."

Pastor Brandon's wife, Nadine, started to disciple a single mom who was a new Christian using the *New Believer's Station* and *Arrival Kit* (developed by Ralph Neighbour, Jr.). Armed with G-12 thinking, they called this meeting a cell group. This single mom now leads the group with Nadine in attendance. A convert from that group is now leading her own group, and the process continues.

The G-12 philosophy reaches down to the training system at NWAC. In the past a person had to be trained before he was allowed to lead a cell. Now people with no training start cells. The rule is: if a cell forms around a person, they must attend the training course. This is not a problem because people want help once they are leading a cell.

Pastor Brandon urges churches to apply the G-12 model to their own unique circumstances. NWAC didn't copy the entire model. They simply adopted those principles that applied best in their own context. Pastor Brandon urges churches to allow the structure to emerge from the grassroots in an environment of listening to the Lord.

HARVEST ASSEMBLY
VIRGINIA BEACH, VA
PASTOR MIKE OSBORN, PART OF THE PASTORAL TEAM
FACTS: 40 CELLS; 500 IN ATTENDANCE

Harvest Assembly, unlike many North American cell churches adopting the G-12 strategy, desires to follow the G-12 model in its entirety. One of the staff members said, "We understand that we must accept the whole package; we cannot pick and choose."[7]

Pastor Mike first heard about the G-12 model in 1997 when César Castellanos spoke in Houston, Texas. Since then, Pastor Mike has devoured everything on the G-12 model and even visited ICM in Bogota. He was so transformed by what he witnessed that he invited several of the ICM pastors to visit Harvest Assembly in order to help in the transition. Harvest Assembly also plans to send more of their key leaders to Bogota in the future.

Harvest Assembly is developing the Encounter Retreats, the School of Leadership, and the follow-up system. They recognize that they must also adopt the values of ICM (e.g., passion for the lost, spiritual warfare, etc.) Pastor Mike has already found his 12 life-long disciples. For some churches, like Harvest Assembly, it may be best to adopt and implement the entire G-12 system.

CENTENNIAL ROAD STANDARD CHURCH
BROCKVILLE, ONTARIO • LAURENCE CROSWELL, SENIOR PASTOR
FACTS: 33 CELLS; 800 SUNDAY ATTENDANCE

Centennial Road Standard Church encourages flexibility with the G-12 model. Each G-12 group is given freedom to develop its own personality. Some G-12 groups meet biweekly, some monthly. Some groups meet in homes, complete with children, others meet in restaurants. Some leaders spend many additional hours shepherding and encouraging their leaders on an individual basis; others do most of their mentoring in the group context. The underlying philosophy is that leaders are unleashed to exercise creativity within the basic structure of the vision.

This Evangelical Methodist Church began transitioning to the cell church model in 1995. The church stagnated at 17 cells and noticed that when the cells multiplied past the third generation, the passion for the vision of cell ministry began to die. It became more and more difficult to motivate people to become interns and some cells keenly felt the wounds of multiplication. Zone Supervisors felt they were further away from "grassroots" ministry and did not necessarily connect with the groups they supervised.

In 1998, Centennial Road transitioned their leadership structure from the 5x5 model to the G-12 model. The senior pastor converted his staff members and spouses into his G-12 group. Pastor Laurence meets with them at 5:30 A.M. every Tuesday morning! From this G-12 hub, seven other G-12 leadership groups have been formed representing a total of 57 leaders.

The church believes that the gentle relational style of the G-12 approach fits their leadership team more effectively than the pyramid management style of the 5x5. The G-12 style has fewer tiers, therefore more people are connected to the hub of the passion for the cell vision.

CORNERSTONE CHURCH
HARRISONBURG, VIRGINIA • PASTOR GERALD MARTIN
FACTS: 75 CELLS; 900 SUNDAY ATTENDANCE

After seven years of experimenting with different cell models, Cornerstone now feels like they've formed their own "saliva" instead of drinking others (This is a term Ralph Neighbour uses to illustrate the absurdity of adopting another church's model and material lock, stock and barrel). Previously, the church felt like David trying to fight in Saul's armor, but now there is a new sense of stability, joy and freedom.

The G-12 model helped Cornerstone reclaim their earlier system. Several years ago, the church organized what they called leadership cells which pastors led. The leadership cell met twice a month. During this time the church had a strong sense of accountability and unity. The weakness was that it put all the leaders in a cell group, which separated them from the normal church members and even led to feelings of elitism. Due to these concerns, the church abandoned the leadership cells, and everyone was encouraged to participate in congregational cells.

Yet, without the accountability provided by the leadership cells, the church seemed to lose its unified sense of direction. When they heard about the G-12 model, it confirmed their former strategy. While adjusting to avoid the earlier errors, Cornerstone adopted a modified G-12 strategy. Now all cell leaders at Cornerstone participate in two cells, one in which they are led and one where they lead. This eliminates the need for zone supervisors. Each cell leader supervises the cell leaders in his cell group and assists them in their ministry.

One unique feature of the G-12 strategy at Cornerstone is that only the cell leader can invite new people to the regular open cell group. If a cell member desires to invite new members, he or she is encouraged to open a new cell group, while continuing to attend the parent cell group.

The G-12 strategy has given Cornerstone unlimited church growth opportunities. Now leaders emerge naturally. Instead of appointing leaders, Cornerstone now simply recognizes leaders when they form a cell group. The 5x5 model hindered the natural progression of leadership, but now Cornerstone releases new leadership in a very natural way. Take the example of a tree. You won't see a tree grunting and groaning to produce growth. It just happens naturally. The G-12 model, in a similar way, has released Cornerstone to grow naturally and continually.

In addition to developing cell leaders, each pastor gives leadership to a ministry department: worship, facilities, prayer, care giving, ministry placement, youth, children and development. Pastor Martin said to me, "Once again the church is united. We are functioning as a team." The vision and direction of the church has been restored. The G-12 strategy has refreshed the church and breathed new life into the cell structure.

CHURCH OF THE NATIONS
ATHENS, GEORGIA • DR. MEL HOLMES
FACTS: 30 CELLS; 1000 SUNDAY ATTENDANCE

The Church of the Nations is an innovative church that is not afraid to change — even if it means paying a high price. For example, when the church transitioned to the cell church philosophy in 1995, 150 people left. Yet, the Church of the Nations continues to grow and reach out to the multi-ethnic melting pot that surrounds the church.

The G-12 strategy helped this church to fine-tune its cell church strategy. Initially, they required all cell leaders to attend both a parent cell and to lead an open cell group. Over time, however, the church discovered that the bonding of a new leader gradually began to move more and more to the cell that he was leading and away from the cell where he had been mentored and parented. Much like children growing up, the felt need for the parent cell began to diminish, as they became more effective parents themselves. Not that the relationship was broken, but like a parent-child relationship, it began to change as the children grew up.

The church leadership discovered that the main issue was not the time constraints of two cells per week but rather trying to maintain meaningful relationships with two separate cell groups (which contained 10 to 12 adults per cell). Over time, this relationship stretching became the primary reason why the church decided to allow individuals to break off from their parent cell and become freestanding cells.

To augment the need for oversight and accountability (especially for those who left the parent cells to become freestanding cell leaders) the church added a Sunday morning cell leader's gathering. This gathering met for one hour prior to the morning worship service. All active leaders attend these sessions in order to receive ministry and ongoing training.

After 18 months, the church did not feel the need to hold this leadership meeting on a weekly basis. Now they meet one Sunday night per month with all the cell leaders. Also, every other week the senior pastor meets with his mentors to encourage and aid them as they mentor the leaders who come to them for support, encouragement and prayer.

The G-12 principles that the Church of the Nations actually follows are:

1. All cell members are taught and expected to be potential leaders. No one is a cell intern. Everyone is a potential leader.
2. The goal is for everyone to disciple 12 people.
3. Cell leaders supervise (disciple) those new leaders that start groups from the parent cell. When all of the cell members become leaders, the parent cell leader meets with all of them at least twice a month, in addition to leading his cell.

4. Everyone is ministered to and then ministers.
5. A person doesn't become a part of your 12 until he or she is leading a cell group.
6. Everyone should win souls and develop potential leaders. Each cell member is encouraged to eventually find his or her "nation" (homogeneous group) that will become his or her 12.
7. The cells no longer multiply by division but rather by replication.

The church no longer appoints section leaders, divisional pastors and zone pastors. They have chosen, rather, to establish "mentors." Dr. Holmes, meets with seven mentors (that will eventually become 12) who in turn meet with their 12. Dr. Holmes says: ". . . relationships never need to be broken, staffing needs remain much lower and no one's potential is stifled."

BETHANY WORLD PRAYER CENTER
BAKER, LOUISIANA • PASTOR LARRY STOCKSTILL
FACTS: 800 CELLS; 8,000 SUNDAY ATTENDANCE

BWPC is the most influential cell church in North America. They hold yearly cell conferences with over 1,000 pastors attending. They've taught thousands of pastors and leaders about cell church ministry.

After Pastor Larry visited ICM in late 1996 with Ralph Neighbour, Jr., he came back intent on transitioning BWPC to the G-12 model. Since 1997, BWPC regularly includes teaching on the G-12 strategy in its annual conferences. Most churches in North America initially heard about the G-12 model from BWPC. Because Bethany's G-12 transition is well documented, I'll limit the information in this section.[8]

At BWPC, every cell member is encouraged to open a cell group and then to continue attending the parent cell group.[9] Billy Hornsby considers this a genuine multiplication in contrast with a division. He explains:

> Other forms of multiplication are by division. One group grows, multiplies by dividing and becomes two. With the principle of 12, groups need not be divided. Simply open more groups with the new leaders that are produced in each circle of 12.[10]

The new group that comes from the parent cell (G-12 group) is called a sub-group. Sub-groups feed the parent G-12 cell. Sub-groups prioritize evangelism, discipleship and feeding the mother G-12 group, while the parent G-12 group focuses on edification, leadership development and multiplication. The sub-group uses approved material that applies to its particular members, while the parent G-12 group always follows the prepared cell lesson.[11]

Like ICM, Bethany believes that every person has the anointing for multiplication. Everyone is expected to enter the equipping track to eventually lead a cell group.

BWPC realizes that flexibility must be built into the G-12 model. BWPC, for example, asks new leaders to return each week to the parent cell group. Yet, there is some elasticity in its model as well. Pastor Hornsby writes:

> We have also discovered that after someone in your group starts a cell group he needs close encouragement that the mentor group provides. However, after several months, he may not need to attend every week but should attend once or twice a month. Though not official, we allow this to take place but know that two meetings a week is premium.[12]

Each parent cell leader, in other words, must discern how to best minister to the ministers (new cell leaders). A G-12 leader, for example, might more effectively minister to the new disciple through individual meetings, phone calls, or notes in the mail rather than simply asking the person to return to the parent cell each week.

Pastor Stockstill also clarifies that the G-12 strategy is more of a principle than a model. During the November 1998 Bethany Cell Church Conference, Larry said:

> The principle of 12 is a concept; it's not a method. What they do in Bogota might be different from what we do in the United States . . . I want you to understand that the principle of the 12 is not a cell principle only, it's a leadership development principle. But we use it with cells.[13]

G-12 principles have transformed Bethany's cell system in several ways: their cells are more homogeneous, their training track incorporates retreats and multiplication flows more naturally. It has provided BWPC with more flexibility and helped them to hold the harvest.

WILL IT WORK IN AMERICA?

Jeannette Buller wondered if the G-12 model would work in the North American context. The above churches demonstrate that it does. These churches discovered new energy for cell multiplication and leadership development by using this strategy. G-12 principles invigorated these churches with fresh creativity and in several cases, revived stagnate cell structures.

G-12 Principles from
International Churches

In the 1800's, the novelist Jules Verne wrote about the challenge of going around the world in 80 days. Yet now with a modem you can circumnavigate the globe from your desktop in 80 seconds or less. Technology has transformed us into an interconnected global village.[1]

Because of this day of global communications, cell churches worldwide can link together in order to share ideas. In this chapter, we'll look at four international cell churches that have applied G-12 principles to their own context.

BERLIN INTERNATIONAL CHURCH
HENRY PAASONEN • C&MA MISSIONARY TO BERLIN, GERMANY
FACTS: CHURCH PLANT

Following unsuccessful attempts to form cells for church planting in Paris, France, Henry Paasonen came upon the G-12 principle while reading a book on the spread of the gospel during Medieval times in Europe. In the book, *How The Irish Saved Civilization* by Thomas Cahill, the author unfolds the story of Ireland's heroic role from the fall of the Roman Empire, through the Dark Ages and to the rise of Medieval Europe.

The second part of the book is largely focused on how the Celtic saints fanned out across the Continent, even into Russia and into the Middle East, and formed monastic communities, which were always purposeful groups of 12. Each member was equipped to be a "warrior monk," much like the members of a G-12 group.

Paasonen writes:

> In reading about these Irish missionary centers and at the same time learning about the work of César Castellanos, my thinking was freed from the spaghetti of accountability lines and levels so often found in various cell models — feedback systems which can become a burden to cell leaders as they are required to attend weekly leadership meetings, maintain shepherding visitation schedules and invest in mentoring relationships. Finally, here was a cell model that functioned as a leadership team, which stayed together rather than splitting to multiply, and which maintained within itself the leadership accountability that in other models stretched over levels and zones.

After seeing four "cell-less" churches planted in the Paris area, Paasonen was transferred to Berlin, Germany. Here, he and the Alliance team in the German capital experienced a breakthrough. They were led to see in Ephesians 4:11-16 cell principles that reflected four essential characteristics of the G-12 model:

1. A cell group designed for cell leaders. Others have noted that these verses call for accountability and intimacy, which can only be met in a cell group. But these verses also identify four members (v.11) as the initial group and as the minimum size of the cell — a quartet of equippers who become the leadership nucleus as the cell grows.
2. A continuity of teamwork required of that quartet a solidarity that calls for it to remain together as a unit and not to split up in the process of cell multiplication.
3. A leadership equipping purpose for that quartet as it mentors others who are brought into the cell and equip them to be cell leaders in their turn.
4. A set of four leadership development tracks suggested in verses 12-16.

The vision for the *Diamond Four* (D-4) model was born! While reflecting key G-12 principles, this humbler model called for an initial growth goal not of 12 members but of only four members — four being the smallest number for a functional cell. For reference purposes, the quartet members have been tentatively designated as the equipper (the apostle), the edifier (the prophet), the evangelist, and the enabler (the pastor/teacher).

Paasonen notes, "Our purpose has been not to slavishly copy the G-12 model but to identify key principles for cell church development natural to the European context." The result has been most encouraging on a European field where higher membership goals, as with the G-12 model, are not easily achieved. Because of the lower responsiveness in a post-modern urban center like Berlin (when compared to Singapore or Colombia), D-4 cell membership is not only more readily achieved but also more intensely concentrated for leadership training. The D-4 cell can then proudly celebrate becoming a completed group at four members and at the same time strive to become the nucleus for a larger cell growing around it as others are added.

In addition to the issue of lower responsiveness, Paasonen tells of another breakthrough in cell growth in the urban centers of Europe: Few professional men or women in a city like Berlin have the time or the energy to be a cell leader following cell leadership models which often burden a cell leader with pastoral responsibilities, with organization of outreach efforts, with concentration on discipleship or mentoring and with maintenance of multiple leadership accountability.

Yet a cell model need not discriminate against such highly active people and keep them out of full participation in cell leadership. When the cell leader role is shared as in the D-4 model, the burden is spread out and the spiritual gifts of each leader are more fully honored.

As in the G-12 model, the D-4 cell is totally concentrated on leadership development and on cell multiplication. Such cell extension is triggered in the sending out of new D-4 cells:

1. An original D-4 is formed to bring at least four men/women to Christ.
2. This carefully chosen quartet is first mentored along the four discipleship tracks suggested in Ephesians 4:12-16.
3. When the prototype has completed its formation, others are brought in around the D-4 nucleus and are invited to form into new D-4 groups.
4. As each new D-4 concludes equipping for discipleship and leadership roles, the members, are sent out as a team to be the nucleus of a new cell. Multiplication is by leadership teams, not by sending out heroic cell leaders.
5. As in the G-12 model, the original D-4 as well as each new D-4 remains together as a continuing quartet. Thus the extension of

such smaller leadership groups can bring about far more explosive growth than in models requiring three times more people in a cell.

6. While continuing to serve together as a D-4 quartet, each cell elects one of its members as coordinator. He or she then reports to an elected pastoral council that administers the whole cell church of D-4 groups. The council in turn elects a senior pastor. No democratic deficit in this model!

In sum, everyone is someone who can mature into D-4 leadership. Everyone can be sent out as part of a team. Everyone can share in the leadership nucleus of a new cell.

The Berlin missionary team calls this strategy Operation Strawberry because a strawberry patch grows by sending out "runners" which then put down roots and grow new plants. Paasonen says, "The runner function is the key — runners holding within themselves all the potential for a new plant." In the same way, one D-4 plant sends out second-generation D-4 runners that have all the potential to start a new D-4 plant. He concludes, "The growing and the going out of D-4 runners as prepared teams is what it's all about!"

LITTLE FALLS CHRISTIAN CENTRE
LITTLE FALLS ROODEPOORT, SOUTH AFRICA
PASTOR HAROLD F. WEITSZ
FACTS: 240 CELLS; 3,000 SUNDAY ATTENDANCE

Have you ever heard of the J-12 model? If you visit Little Falls Christian Centre, you'll hear about it a lot. This creative church actually mixed the 5x5 and the G-12 models into a new synergy called the J-12 model. After analyzing the strengths and weaknesses of both models, they realized that neither one was perfect.

The old saying, "If it's not broken, don't fix it" highlights why

LFCC didn't adopt the entire G-12 model. The church had experienced continual growth for the last couple years. The leadership didn't feel the *need* to make radical changes to the pastoral care system, but they did find some G-12 concepts that would improve the system.

They also examined their local context, which was very similar to a fast-paced North American lifestyle. They decided that the pure G-12 model (with two or three meetings per week) would not work in their busy society.

The G-12 model, however, has impacted LFCC in several key areas: First, Little Falls now seeks to develop each cell member into a cell leader, based on the premise that every Christian can reach at least 12 people in a lifetime. Major emphasis is therefore placed on quality leadership development.

Second, leaders are released more rapidly to grow new cells. If you want to grow the church, you add new members. But if you want to multiply the church growth-rate, you have to multiply leaders. The church is promoting new cell planting in addition to normal cell multiplication.

Third, LFCC now multiplies its cells at 12 instead of 15. The average cell size of the church is 10, and the lower target of 12 for multiplication is reached much easier. Fewer communication lines in smaller cells make them more effective, and better cell member participation is also achieved.

Fourth, LFCC has tweaked its leadership training to produce new leaders at an astonishing rate of four months. The focus on leadership development of the G-12 was the cause for the development of the new training track at LFCC.[2] The continuous shortage of new leaders for cell multiplication or planting has effectively been solved. The launching of many new leaders has resulted in accelerated church growth.

By lowering the cell multiplication number and speeding up the training of new leaders, LFCC's J-12 system is bearing much fruit.

In summary, the church uses the number 12, and the basics of the G-12 training system and its encounters, but it continues to use the Jethro system (5x5) of cell structure through its various levels of Cell leaders, Zone Supervisors, Zone Pastors and District Pastors.

ABBALOVE CHURCH
JAKARTA, INDONESIA • PASTOR EDDY LEO
FACTS: 510 CELLS, 6,000 SUNDAY ATTENDANCE

Pastor Eddy Leo is one of the leaders of Abbalove, a rapidly growing cell church in Jakarta, Indonesia. The way Abbalove is currently carrying out its follow-up and leadership development is particularly exciting.[3]

Follow-up
After Eddy Leo visited ICM in Bogota, he concluded that the growth at ICM was more a result of the excellent follow-up system than of the G-12 model.

Prior to February 1999, Abbalove retained about 20% of those responding to the Gospel. Since making follow-up a priority, this rate has shot up to 33%. 800 of the 2,400 who have responded so far this year are now consistent cell members. Since December 1998, Abbalove has seen about 100 new people coming to Christ every Sunday. The primary means of harvesting is large gatherings, such as the Sunday Celebrations. This year every message preached contains the Gospel.

What Abbalove does now is very similar to what's happening at ICM. Immediately after making a public response at a large gathering, a newcomer is ushered in to the Welcome Room where a counselor discusses with him or her assurance of salvation. Before the newcomer's address is recorded, the counselor asks if there is any need for which the newcomer would like prayer. This focus on praying for felt needs becomes the initial link for follow-up. The newcomer is handed a card on which to write his need and address. The new Christian is asked if it would be appropriate for someone to come and visit them. If he or she answers, "Yes," the completed card is given to the cell group that meets nearest his or her home.

That very same week the cell group prays for the new convert in their district, and then a cell member contacts that person, asking about his or her need and saying they are praying and would like to visit. Normally, if someone other than the friend who brought him or her to church were to try and visit, they would be rejected. But because the focus is on caring for felt needs, the door is opened.

Generally four visits are made in the first four weeks, with the cell member explaining how to grow in Christ, and inviting the new convert to the cell group. The newcomer is then invited to an 18-lesson new believer's class that continues year round. The objective is not to complete a course but to achieve the following goals:

1. Assurance of salvation
2. Deliverance and healing from past problems
3. Water Baptism
4. Filling/baptism in the Holy Spirit
5. Establish a spiritual devotional life: quiet time, prayer, etc.
6. Changing of basic values

In the middle of each series a spiritual Encounter Retreat is held, outside the city, where six of the 18 lessons are covered. Along with the lesson, many are filled with the Spirit and delivered from past bondage. Every new believer must attend one such retreat. Usually about a third of those attending are mentors or sponsors. About 50 people attend each retreat. While the Encounter weekends are running, a team of intercessors is praying. Since initiating this follow-up approach earlier this year, they are seeing results. Most of those who attend the retreats continue in their Christian commitment.

Leadership Development

For the previous three years, Abbalove plateaued at 430-460 cell groups. There were two reasons for this. First, no leaders were forthcoming. People simply didn't have the vision. Second, groups didn't like the feeling of divorce that accompanied cell multiplication.

Since visiting Bogota, Eddy and his co-leaders have adopted the *vision* of the Groups of 12 model, but *not* the *strategy*. They now teach the whole congregation that every member must become like Jesus — their character should become like Jesus', they must become a leader like Jesus and they are to reproduce themselves in 12 others like Jesus.

But while this *philosophy* is similar to the church in Bogota, the *method* of implementing it is very different!

Previously, Abbalove was structured very similar to the Groups of 12 model. Everything was structured in a vertical, hierarchical structure in which every member of a cell also led a cell whose members in turn led new cells. Because of problems with the former *vertical* model, Abbalove decided to adopt a *horizontal* approach to cell ministry.[4] The lifecycle of each cell group is now divided into 4 stages; infant, child, youth and adult.

Infant Stage (2-3 months)

The focus during this stage is on bonding relationships and on praying for new leaders. Every cell member is asked, "When do you want to become a leader?" If the answer is "Two years from now" this is written down. The cell leader then asks, "How can I help you become a leader?" During the following stages he/she then focuses on those who are more ready to become leaders.

Child Stage (2-3 months)

The cell leader spends this next period discipling the potential leaders in the cell. Usually, the cell leader meets with the core team for 30-45 minutes after each cell meeting to disciple them. He or she will train them in the areas of faithfulness, prayer, Bible study, fellowship and evangelism.

Youth Stage (2-3 months)

At this point, the cell members are divided so each member of the core team can care for others within the cell. Cell meetings now consist of two sections. The first hour is similar to a normal cell meeting. During the second hour, potential leaders meet with new prospective leaders whom they have spotted or brought to the group, teaching them the same basic material.

Adult Stage (2-3 months)

This is the testing stage, in which the potential leaders (from the *child stage*) direct their own sub-groups (from the *youth stage*) as a cell group on a separate day, with the cell leaders overseeing (usually by visiting 2 new cells each week). The new leaders are encouraged to attend both the new cell group and the mother cell during this stage. If one of the new cells is not functioning well, they can return to the mother cell for a while longer. Once the new cells are functioning comfortably, the mother cell stops meeting.

In this way, one cell can multiply in one year not into two new cells, but into as many cells as there are sub-groups. Zone supervisors, as in the 5x5 model, supervise these new cells. The original cell leader leads one of the new cells, continuing on until he/she has produced 12 leaders.

Not only does this approach deliberately raise up more leaders in a gentle way, but the gradual birthing of smaller sub-groups within the group alleviates the problem of a painful separation once the cell reaches a certain number of people.

The results have been encouraging thus far for Abbalove. Since February 1999, Abbalove has grown from 450 to 510 cell groups. Now many people want to be leaders! There is fresh vision within the cells! This system is purpose oriented rather than materials oriented. While the central leadership team gives guidance, each congregation and zone has freedom to develop its own methods in order to achieve the purpose.

THE CHRISTIAN CENTER OF GUAYAQUIL
GUAYAQUIL, ECUADOR
PASTOR JERRY SMITH
FACTS: 1,900 CELLS; 6,500 SUNDAY ATTENDANCE

I first visited CCG in 1996. At that time, the church faithfully followed the classic 5x5 model and had grown to become the largest church in Ecuador. Yet, when pastor Smith witnessed the explosive growth in Bogota, he decided to completely adopt the G-12 model. CCG has sent well over 50 pastors and leaders to Bogota to understand the G-12 model and then to fully implement it at CCG. Expressing his commitment to fully transition to the G-12 model, Smith wrote to Ralph Neighbour, Jr. saying, "We are still struggling with the transition, although there is *no turning back* nor doubting what we are going to do, with God's grace and help."[5]

CCG initially transitioned to the G-12 model by assigning everyone a ministry. Former district pastor, Johnny Ascenso became head of the young people's department. District Pastor Inez Aguello was placed over the women and young women professionals. Others opened different ministries. Like ICM, the church required each person to have a ministry in the church.

The first time I visited CCG in 1996, its cell group divisions looked like this:

DISTRICTS	CELL GROUPS	ATTENDANCE
District One	602	3,892
District Two	442	3,331
District Three	543	3,530
Total:	1,587	10,753

After initiating its transition, its cell divisions looked like this:

TYPE OF CELL GROUP	NUMBER OF CELL GROUPS	ATTENDANCE IN CELL GROUPS
CHILDREN	171	1,047
JUNIORS	83	382
YOUNG PEOPLE	79	372
WOMEN	11	30
MEN	27	140
PROFESSIONAL WOMEN	20	116
PROFESSIONAL MEN	17	49
COUPLES	18	118
CONSOLIDATION	15	78
WORSHIP	21	152
PRAYER	91	572
CONSERVATION	19	130
MINISTRY OF CHRIST	24	1,255
ADDICTIONS	0	0
HIGH SCHOOL CELLS (Required for Parents)	249	1,375
ADMINISTRATION	15	58
GEOGRAPHICAL ZONE CELLS	635	2,672
SATELLITE CELLS	343	1,781
TOTAL	1,838	10,327

CCG decided to run its cell groups based on homogeneous ministerial categories, although Pastor Smith told me that the geographical distinctions would continue because they make it easier to place new Christians in cells.[6]

CCG asks all cell leaders to commit themselves to three meetings per week. Each cell leader meets with his or her G-12 leader (first meeting), meets with his own G-12 members (second meeting) and leads an open cell group (third meeting).

CCG has patterned its leadership training after ICM in Bogota. It holds similar Encounter Retreats and like ICM, their School of Leadership lasts nine months (three trimesters).[7] CCG has radically changed to embrace the G-12 model.

PUTTING THE PIECES TOGETHER

We've analyzed four different approaches to the G-12 strategy from four distinct churches on four diverse continents. Henry Paasonen transformed the G-12 model into a new package called the D-4 model — a better fit for the post-modern culture of Berlin, Germany. Across the globe in South Africa, Pastor Harold Weitsz and the LFCC staff combined the G-12 model with their 5x5 structure, even calling it the J-12 model. In Indonesia, the Abbalove Church has effectively used G-12 principles to transform their follow-up and cell reproduction. Jerry Smith and CCG, on the other hand, purposely followed the G-12 model in its entirety.

Chapter 12 will synthesize the patterns and principles that have emerged from the North American churches as well as the International churches.

APPLYING G-12 PRINCIPLES
TO YOUR CHURCH

In the Introduction, I mentioned a pastor who visited ICM and then returned to his church to implement the entire system. His new fire was snuffed out by reality, and he quickly learned that his vision to be like ICM was impossible. But there is good news. He learned from his failure. He learned that he first needed to introduce basic cell church values before jumping into the G-12 model. Although hard to accept, he had to admit that he had fallen into the trap of copying a model instead of adopting the principles.

To correct these errors, he analyzed his own context and decided to implement only the G-12 principles that best fit his own church. He used G-12 principles of every member as a potential leader, every leader a potential supervisor, and he even organized his training track with G-12 principles in mind. Now he is on the right track.

THE TRANSFERABLE PRINCIPLES OF THE G-12 MODEL

Some G-12 principles are more desirable than others. Churches, in other words, have repeatedly chosen to adopt certain principles and exclude others. The following principles will help you in your G-12 journey.

Flexibility in Cell Multiplication

Freedom. The G-12 model provides freedom for cell churches accustomed to one style of cell multiplication. When I first visited Bethany World Prayer Center in 1996, it had topped out at just over 300 cell groups. Now it is closing in on 900 cell groups. The G-12 model provided Bethany with the freedom to innovate and experiment with homogeneous categories and new ways to start cell groups.

For New Market Alliance Church and Faith Community Church, the G-12 model helped them catch a vision for cell planting — starting cells whenever there was a trained leader and at least one other person. The focus on smaller cells and tapping into the potential of every cell member stirred Henry Paasonen to develop the D-4 model. Tim Scheuer of the Church Army writes, "There are more ways to start groups, greater variety in who leads them and freedom in when they meet. Now groups can start wherever and however."[1]

Most churches liked the G-12 principle that cells can start whenever there is a trained leader. This liberated them from waiting for a particular number in order to divide into two groups. These churches discarded the traditional form of mother-daughter multiplication. Rather, the G-12 philosophy provided them with additional, creative options.

Every Person a Potential Leader

One of the most liberating principles of the G-12 philosophy is that every member is a potential cell leader. Many churches are simply discarding titles such as cell intern or cell assistant, and are instead calling each member a potential leader. The new thinking is that everyone is in the process of becoming a cell leader. For some churches, this new vision has caused them to streamline their training systems. Instead of having a training track for each position (cell member, cell intern, cell leader, etc.) churches are simplifying their training to equip each member to lead cell groups and supervise others.

Maintenance of Relationships

Several churches were attracted to the G-12 model because the relationship is maintained between parent and daughter cell. Again, this brings new freedom and simplicity by asking each parent cell leader to maintain an intimate relationship with the new cell leader. Faith Community Church, for example, now asks each new church member to immediately receive discipleship in a small group, to prepare to disciple others by leading a small group and to eventually disciple those who are discipling others (supervision of other cell leaders). Notice the continuity of relationship — the parent cell leader maintains relationships with the new cell leaders.

Ministry to the Ministers

Most of the case study churches wisely looked beyond the methodology of a certain number of meetings to the principle of ministering to the ministers. These churches realized that real world ministry requires adjustments. When Pastor Tim Scheuer noticed that time and distance foiled his demand for two meetings per week, he looked for creative alternatives. He focused on the principle of ministering to the ministers rather than the method of two nights per week. The Church of the Nations, on the other hand, discovered that developing two sets of relationships (parent cell and daughter cell) overwhelmed some cell leaders; therefore the church developed creative alternatives in order to continue ministering to the ministers.

Actually, the question of a set number of meetings has caused many churches to reject the G-12 concept outright. Yet, there is an emerging consensus that emphasizes the principle of satisfying the needs of the new leader, rather than stacking on additional meetings. As long as new cell leaders receive ministry by the parent cell leader, the number of meetings is less important.

Less Hierarchical Structure Is Preferable

Many of the churches liked the flexibility and creativity of the G-12 model. It helped them to structure their cells along relational lines, such as homogeneous groups. For these churches, the G-12 strategy liberated them from a top-heavy hierarchy that weighed them down rather than lifting them up.

Leaders Must Maintain Involvement in Ministry

The G-12 strategy has encouraged several of the case study churches to keep their cell leaders actively involved. Some churches are discovering that removing supervisors from direct involvement in the cell group causes stagnation. Following the G-12 pattern, many churches require their cell leaders to stay actively involved in leading a cell group, even after forming their G-12 groups.

Another attractive feature is that the G-12 model requires less staff relationships. Pastor Jerry Smith wrote this e-mail immediately after his church's annual cell church conference in which César Castellanos was the main speaker:

I do not plan to keep pastors on staff that have less than 50 cell groups as of June 30, 1998, with a couple of exceptions. I would like to follow their [ICM] model. Leaders with 250 cell groups come on staff with one-half salary. To add additional pastors on staff, [ICM] expects them to have 500 cell groups, with at least 6 people attending.[2]

Streamlined Training that Focuses on Concentrated Ministry
The G-12 model helped nearly all of the churches to streamline their training tracks and to emphasize concentrated ministry and teaching in a retreat format.[3]

REINVENTION

The science of change teaches that new ideas and concepts are seldom taken as is.[4] People reinvent them to make them their own. This is certainly true with regard to the G-12 model. Few churches chose to adopt the entire G-12 model. The majority preferred to reinvent this model according to their own circumstances and felt needs. The G-12 strategy is such a fluid concept that it is quickly adapting as it changes across different cultures and churches.

Many churches are adapting the composition of their groups in light of learning from the G-12 model. The 5x5 model tended to focus on family groups in a geographical framework. ICM, on the other hand, organizes cells homogeneously. Churches like Bethany World Prayer Center and The Christian Center of Guayaquil are combining their previous geographical systems with a new emphasis on homogeneous groups that are organized according to G-12 principles. Again, churches are reinventing the G-12 model to fit their own situation.

Dave Brandon of Newmarket Alliance in Ontario, Canada, says, "We had been trying to implement the cell model for seven years.

After we learned of the G-12 model, we took key principles from the model, and then we forgot about G-12 and developed our own model."[5] Brandon counsels: "Let the structure emerge from the grass roots."[6] After immersing themselves in seminars, books and interaction with other churches, Brandon's members discovered their own model that fit their particular context. There are no short cuts to this process. You can't copy someone else's model. You must prayerfully reinvent it to fit your own situation.

DON'T FORGET THE CELL CHURCH VALUES

Those at ICM talk constantly about spiritual power, spiritual victories, spiritual liberation and relatively little about "the model." North American churches tend to become enamored with the model. Yet, a church will never get the same results as Bogota by simply copying a model without adopting the values of the church. Tim Scheuer echoes a similar concern: "Many churches want New Testament results without New Testament values. The values are critical. We were doing cells before we heard of the G-12 model, so we had a head start on the values. I don't think it would have worked if we had not already shifted values."[7]

You don't have to travel to Bogota to start structuring your church for increased leadership mobilization. Begin with the G-12 principles and apply them to your own context. Learn from the above 12 churches who have already pioneered new paths using the G-12 model. Steal the best with pride. As you combine these principles with proven cell church values, you will begin to see exciting results.

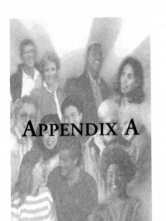

APPENDIX A

HIDDEN DETAILS OF
THE G-12 MODEL

My cousin, Mike, tried for days to fix my worn-out notebook computer, but to no avail. "The registry system in Windows 95 is very complicated," he said. He then proceeded to show me a gigantic book that comprised the Windows 95 registry. With 30,000 lines of computer code, it's best not to touch the registry of Windows 95 unless you know what you're doing. ICM has many layers and details that are not obvious at first glance. This appendix offers insight into the inner workings of the registry of ICM.

MINISTRY DEPARTMENTS AT ICM

At ICM there are a wide variety of ministries. The ministries include: worship, spiritual warfare, counseling, ushers, counseling, follow-up, social action, pastoral care, accounting, video, sound, bookstore and more.

When I first visited ICM in 1996 and 1997, the cell groups and G-12 groups were linked to particular ministries. Cell groups were identified by particular ministries — worship cell groups, usher cell groups, spiritual warfare cell groups and more. Depending on the size and specificity of the ministry, there might be many cell groups or very few. A ministerial department like sound, social action or accounting would have fewer cell groups than the larger ministries such as young people, worship, men's ministry or women's ministry.

Although this was a creative way to organize the cell groups, the wide array of ministries appeared cumbersome and programmatic. I've known pastors who returned from Bogota with a new vision for adding programs (ministries) to their cell church. They came away thinking, "At last, I can be a cell church and have a wide range of ministries. I'm going to start immediately to implement men's ministry, social action and television ministry."

As far as ICM is concerned, the ministries were simply a way to group people together.[1] ICM understood how to sort everything out, but often others do not.

I counsel people not to copy ICM by adding all kinds of ministries. These questions must first be asked:

1. Do you need a new ministry?
2. Can the cells meet the need of this new ministry?
3. How do you plan on integrating this new ministry into the current cell structure?

HOMOGENOUS GROUPINGS

When I visited ICM in 1998 and 1999, the cell groups and G-12 groups were now linked to the homogeneous groupings (men, women, couples, young professionals, youth, adolescents, and children) instead of individual ministry departments.

If you were under men's ministry, all of your disciples would be men. If you were under women's ministry, all of your disciples would be women. In Bogota, if you were a disciple under César Castellanos, your open cell group would probably be all male (although not required anymore). This is the logical progression in the homogeneous category called men at ICM. Why? Because every member of your cell is a potential leader and only cell leaders can be disciples. If you had women attending your men's cell, you couldn't look at them as potential leaders, since you could only supervise (disciple) male leaders.

Only under the couples ministry would you disciple both husband and wife. In this case, you would minister with your wife and the open cell groups would also include both men and women. At ICM, there is no distinction in the youth ministry. Among the young people, a female discipler might have several young men under her. While visiting ICM in 1998, we greeted Joahnna, the oldest daughter of César and Claudia Castellanos, along with her G-12 group. The majority of her disciples were male young people.

The cell church worldwide is learning that strict geographical barriers often hinder instead of strengthen cell ministry. But this argument is equally true with regard to strict homogeneous boundaries, such as men and women. Remember, the thrust of homogenous groups is to encourage growth because of natural groupings. Don't allow your natural groupings to form an iron curtain around your ministry.

I personally don't like the idea of dividing into men's groups or women's groups. It seems too artificial to me. A men's ministry in the church such as Promise Keepers is not bad. But why not allow people to freely gravitate to such groupings instead of insisting on them.

Be especially careful here while your church is transitioning to the G-12 model. I would advise that you don't even mention the men/women dichotomy of Bogota. I view this as something extra.

"But shouldn't men disciple men and women disciple women?" This is a reasonable question. First, you must remember that discipleship in the G-12 system is not intensive one-on-one discipleship. Generally, discipleship occurs at the group level. The G-12 group meets together. Second, the G-12 system emphasizes pastoral care more than intense discipleship. Your training track should provide the lion's share of teaching and equipping. Your G-12 structure provides the care and support, much like the Jethro model.

Luis Salas made it clear that the divisions of men, women and couples are more of a methodology than anything else. He told us that this is unique to Bogota and shouldn't necessarily be followed in every context.[2]

WHEN TO STOP LEADING A CELL GROUP

ICM has wrestled with this question. When I visited ICM in 1997, one of the top leaders insisted that the solution was for everyone to maintain an open cell. This was the official answer being propagated among the young people at that time. It was a simple matter of adding another meeting to an already crowded agenda.

The more recent line of thinking (as discussed in Chapter Four) is that you continue leading an open cell group until you have your 144, that is, until each of your 12 has also found their 12. But until then, you continue to lead an open cell in order to continue making disciples (producing new leaders). You would pass down these new disciples to the 12 under you until each one of them has formed his 12.[3]

In our adaptation of the G-12 model, I maintain my cell group, while supervising those from my cell group who have opened their own group. I must supervise the cell leaders who have started groups from my cell group, but I also maintain my open group.

Now, it's true that most churches that have adopted the G-12 model will tell you that once you've found your 12 disciples, you no longer need to have an open cell group. Reflecting this thinking, Randall Neighbour writes,

> When you have up to 12 couples (working as one) or individuals with their own groups meeting on another evening apart from your meeting with them, you will have a group of 12 and you can close it. New believers you personally reach for Christ will stay in your original group for a couple of weeks and go into one of your member's groups.[4]

I'd prefer for someone to maintain an open cell group and meet with their 12 bimonthly or monthly than to stop leading a cell group. Open cells are the life of the cell church, and I recommend that all leaders direct one. Without leading an open cell group, you can lose touch with the very heart of the cell church.

The suggestion by Randall that conversions from the G-12 group would be passed down to the 12 disciples also has its problems. As Mike Atkins, former senior pastor of Church of the Nations in Athens, Georgia, says:

> . . . individuals who are led to Christ by one person may actually be discipled and mentored by someone unrelated to that individual. This can bring up the tension of a lack of homogeneity if a cell that matches the individual's station in life, economic level or personal needs cannot be found.[5]

CONFUSING **G-12** WITH OTHER AREAS OF **ICM**

ICM has an excellent equipping track, but so do many other cell churches around the world. Don't confuse the G-12 model with the equipping track. The G-12 model is a care system for those who have passed through the equipping track; it's not the equipping track. Training cell leadership is different from the G-12 model. Alan Creech writes:

> I think some of the confusion about this Principle of 12 is happening because we are mixing up a system with a theology. What I mean is that just because César Castellanos takes his people on a "clean-up" retreat, . . . that doesn't mean that we have to, nor does it really have anything to do with the model of the Principle of 12.[6]

Each cell church trains their future leaders specifically, but leadership training is distinct from the G-12 model. The equipping track must be dedicated to one thing: equipping. Don't expect higher levels of training to emerge from your G-12 system. You'll be disappointed.

NOTES

INTRODUCTION

[1] I'm referring to Christian Center of Guayaquil (2,000 cells and 7,000 in attendance), Bethany World Prayer Center (over 800 cells and 8,000 in attendance), Living Water Church (900 cells, 9,000 in attendance), and ICM itself.

[2] Jim Egli, "What Do I Do with the G-12 Model?" *CellChurch* Vol. 7, no. 4 (Fall 1998): 26-27.

[3] César Castellanos, *Sueña y Ganarás el Mundo* (Bogota, Colombia: Vilit Editorial, 1998), 86.

[4] César Castellanos, *Successful Leadership through the G-12 Model,* audiotape of lecture presented at the Fourth Convention of Multiplication and Revival, January 1999.

[5] Ibid.

[6] César Castellanos, *The Cell Method through the Groups of Twelve,* audiotape of message presented at Living Water in Lima, Perú, March 1998. With regard to holding people responsible, I've discovered that this is true. Before starting the G-12 system in our church, I was the director of a zone, with 25 cell groups. I felt responsible to care for the new leaders. "After all, I'm the director," I told myself. After our church started the G-12 philosophy, I changed my philosophy. I expected that each leader take full responsibility to meet regularly with those disciples under his or her care. The G-12 model helped me pass the baton of accountability and pastoral care to my cell leaders. It will help you do the same.

[7] My research of ICM includes four visits, watching 12 video tapes, listening to 24 audio tapes, studying all of their primary Spanish literature, attending many of their services,

administrating a 29-question survey to many of their cell leaders and interviews with a large number of their top leadership. Probably the most important part of my G-12 education was actually participating as a pastor in a transition to the G-12 model, since at that time I was able to wrestle with the G-12 principles on a personal level.

CHAPTER 1

[1] Patrick Johnstone, *Operation World* (Grand Rapids, MI: Zondervan Publishing House, 1993), p. 174.

[2] It's amazing how that all of his family has now come to Christ and a large number of them now work in at ICM. At first he had to separate from them, but then both César and Claudia Castellanos began to pray for them. Through fervent prayer, they received Jesus.

[3] César Castellanos, *El Fundamento de la Palabra* (Bogota, Colombia: Editorial Vilit, 1999), p. 53.

[4] Castellanos, *Sueña y Ganarás el Mundo*, pp. 11-12.

[5] "Tent Of Meeting in Print" (May - August 1997) "This article was published in *Joy Magazine* (July 1997), 4. Submitted with permission for Internet publication obtained from Peter Wreford, the editor (editor.newlife@hertz.ukonline.co.uk) July 31, 1997. Editorial Office: New Life Publishing Co., PO Box 64, Rotherham, South Yorkshire S60 2YT.

[6] César Castellanos, "Exploring the Groups of Twelve," interview by Jim Egli, *CellChurch* Vol. 7, no. 2 (Spring 1998): 24.

[7] Ibid.

[8] Ibid.

[9] Ibid.

[10] César Castellanos, *Successful Leadership through the G-12 Model*, audiotape.

[11] César Castellanos, "Exploring the Groups of Twelve," 24.

[12] César Castellanos, *Sueña y Ganarás el Mundo*, 68.

[13] Ibid., 69

[14] César Fajardo not only initiated the first successful G-12 groups at ICM, he also established the follow-up system (consolidation) and the Encounter Retreats. It's well known that the ministry of the young people is the most successful at ICM.

[15] César Castellanos, "Exploring the Groups of Twelve," 24.

[16] When I was present in April 1999, there were 18,000 in the Saturday young people's service, about 17,000 in the Sunday morning services, and perhaps 7,000 in the ten satellite churches throughout Bogota. This would total 42,000. Because I don't have scientific figures for the satellite churches and it's hard to count precisely in an indoor stadium, I've rounded off the attendance figure at 45,000 as of April 1999. At this time, ICM views the Saturday night service as an independent service and doesn't expect those on Saturday to attend the Sunday worship services.

[17] César Castellanos, *Sueña y Ganarás el Mundo*, 87.

[18] "Tent Of Meeting in Print," 4.

[19] César Castellanos, *Sueña y Ganarás el Mundo*, 38.

[20] Unknown source. I discovered this poem and wrote it down while attending Prairie Bible Institute in Alberta, Canada in 1979.

CHAPTER 2

[1] César Fajardo, *Commit Your Life to the Divine Vision*, audiotape of lecture presented at the Fourth Convention of Multiplication and Revival, January 1999.

[2] César Castellanos, *Successful Leadership through the G-12 Model*, audiotape.

[3] César Castellanos, *Anointing for Multiplication*, audiotape of message presented at Bethany World Prayer Center, November 1997.

[4] In 1996, for example, the cells were organized around different ministries (e.g., cells of worship, cells of spiritual warfare, etc.). In 1997, they reorganized the cells around homogeneous categories (e.g., men's cells, women's cells, etc.).

[5] Frank Gonzalez, *What is a Cell Group?* audiotape of lecture presented at the Fourth Convention of Multiplication and Revival, January 1999.

[6] *The American Heritage® Dictionary of the English Language*, 3rd ed., s.v. "spirituality."

[7] Days before I arrived in Colombia, the guerrillas had kidnapped 70 people. The church responded by praying for 24 hours straight over their national radio station.

[8] César Castellanos, *Sueña y Ganarás el Mundo*, 91.

[9] César Castellanos, cell seminar in May 1998 in Quito, Ecuador.

[10] Freddy Rodriguez, *A Successful Cell Vision*, videotape of lecture presented at the 1996 Cell Church Conference in Bogota, Colombia, 1996.

[11] To arrive at the position of assistant prayer leader, for example, you must have undertaken five three-day fasts, while the position of prayer group leader is reserved for those who have undertaken three 40-day fasts.

[12] In these long fasts, the norm is to fast during the day and then to eat at night.

[13] Granted, this characteristic doesn't come naturally to North American leadership. And yes, I'm willing to concede that Latin leadership is more authoritarian and submission comes more readily in the Latin culture. Regardless of the culture, however, submission, like oil, relieves friction in the G-12 system, and one does well to recognize this principle.

[14] Jorge Lopez, *El Perfil de un Líder* (Fraternidad Cristiana de Guatemala, Guatemala, n.d.), 1.

[15] Among the young people, a leader of a cell group who also has a disciple(s) under him is expected to attend at least six meetings per week: his own cell, meeting with his disciples, meeting with his discipler, part of the leadership school, the youth service, and the Sunday morning worship service.

The leaders under the worship department were encouraged to lead three cell groups per week, attend the Thursday worship time, the Sunday service, etc. I attended one cell leadership training class in which it was announced that only those who were leading three cell groups would have the privilege to attend a special retreat.

[16] Mike Osborn, "The Heart Behind Cells" *CellChurch* Vol. 8, no.1 (Winter 1999): 26.

[17] It seems that certain leaders are now recognizing that if they are not careful, burn out could result.

[18] James C. Collins & Jerry I. Porras, *Built to Last: Successful Habits of Visionary Companies* (New York: Harper Collins Publishers, 1994), 121.

[19] Ibid., 132.

[20] César Castellanos, *Successful Leadership through the G-12 Model*, audiotape.

[21] Ibid.

[22] Ibid.

[23] Ibid.

[24] César Fajardo, *A Successful Cell Vision*, videotape of lecture presented at the ICM conference in Bogota, 1996.

[25] César Fajardo, *The Vision*, audiotape of lecture presented at the Fourth Convention of Multiplication and Revival, January 1999.

[26] "Tent Of Meeting in Print," 4.

[27] César Castellanos, *10 Commandments for Cell Group*, videotape of lecture presented at the ICM conference in Bogota, 1997.

[28] César Castellanos, *Transitioning to the Cell Church Philosophy*, audiotape of lecture presented at the Fourth Convention of Multiplication and Revival, January 1999.

[29] César Castellanos, *Sueña y Ganarás el Mundo*, 172.

[30] Ibid., 174.

[31] Ibid., 175.

[32] César Catellanos, videotape of cell seminar presented in Quito, Ecuador, May 1998.

[33] César Castellanos, *Sueña y Ganarás el Mundo*, 174.

[34] Richard B. Wilke, *And Are We Yet Alive?* (Nashville, TN: Abingdon Press, 1986), 59.

[35] César Castellanos, *Anointing for Multiplication*, audiotape of lecture presented at Bethany World Prayer Center, November 1997.

[36] I have a tremendous respect for Claudia Castellanos. She clearly explains the G-12 and cell vision. She's an excellent speaker and a very gracious person. I've had the privilege of spending quality time with her in 1996 when she graciously explained to me the vision of ICM.

[37] Several of Pastor Castellano's family members fill staff positions. In 1996, I personally talked with two sisters, two brothers, and the mother of Pastor Castellanos before initially talking with Pastor Castellanos. Several in the family of Claudia Castellanos (pastor's wife) also hold key positions in the church.

[38] César Castellanos, *Sueña y Ganarás el Mundo*, 84.

[39] Claudia Castellanos, videotape of cell seminar presented in Quito, Ecuador, May 1998.

[40] Ibid.

[41] César Castellanos, *Sueña y Ganarás el Mundo*, 169.

[42] Ibid., 87.

[43] Ibid., 165.

[44] Ibid., 166. César recalls one leader saying. "I'm grieved pastor because I can't leave the cell church vision."

[45] Ibid.

[46] César Castellanos, *10 Commandments for Cell Group*, videotape.

CHAPTER 3

[1] This was the statistical breakdown of the cell groups in 1998:

Cells among Young People in Mother Church	6,500 cell groups
Additional Homogeneous Cells in Mother Church	11,500 cell groups
Cells in Satellite Churches	6,000 cell groups
Total Cell Groups	24,000 cell groups

In March 1999, ICM revealed that they had closed 6,000 cell groups that were very small, or only existed on paper. They are trying to start stronger cells, with at least six people.

[2] César Castellanos, *10 Commandments for Cell Group*, videotape.

[3] Claudia Patricia Lorelli, the main worship leader at ICM, teaches people that each cell is a small church and the leader watches over the people in that church. The leader prepares all week to satisfy the needs of each cell member. He or she edifies and pastors the people. The leader calls the people to the cell. He bears the burden of all the cell leaders (*Cells: The Backbone of the Church*, audiotape of lecture presented at the Fourth Convention of Multiplication and Revival, January 1999). The cell leader at ICM is even instructed to know the financial situation of the members. At the same time, the cell leaders are strictly forbidden to lend money.

[4] César Castellanos, "Exploring the Groups of Twelve," 24.

[5] César Castellanos, *Transitioning to the Cell Church Philosophy*, audiotape.

[6] Frank Gonzalez, *What is a Cell Group?*, audiotape.

[7] César Castellanos, *Transitioning to the Cell Church Philosophy*, audiotape.

[8] Ibid.

[9] Ricardo's example is very common at ICM. I could not believe it when one of the budding leaders among the professionals told me that he planned to personally lead 12 groups, while he slowly delegated them to his disciples. Although many of the cells are weak and small, the emphasis on multiplication helps the leader to develop important skills, evangelize friends and family, and care for the church at large.

[10] Eddie, one of 12 of Freddy Rodriguez, interview by author, May 1998.

CHAPTER 4

[1] Granted, the G-12 system has already been adapted to fit the North American culture, and most adaptations don't require three separate meetings. The discipleship time at Bethany World Prayer Center, for example, takes place in the parent cell. At Bethany new cell leaders direct their own group and also attend the parent cell each week. In this way, multiplication takes place without division. While BWPC has successfully reduced the number of meetings from three to two, it's doubtful that in-depth discipleship takes place in the context of a normal home cell group meeting. A normal cell meeting focuses on edification rather than in-depth discipleship. In some cases the new leaders meets with the parent cell leader one-half hour before the meeting starts, but this is not a

requirement (more on Bethany World Prayer Center in chapter 10).

[2] Until recently, those cell leaders under the men's homogeneous department could only lead all male cell groups. As of March 1999, ICM relaxed this rule and once again the cell groups under men's network can be heterogeneous. However, if a male disciple is under the network of César Castellanos, he can only include other males in his G-12 group.

[3] César Farjado, email to author, 1 December, 1998.

[4] César Castellanos, *The Cell Method through the Groups of Twelve*, audiotape. At times, it appears that ICM teaches that each person "picks" his disciples subjectively, according to various characteristics in the potential disciple. I talked to one leader who told me that he had seven disciples, but that only three of them were actually leading cell groups. The other four were in the process of becoming cell leaders. Admittedly, this is a confusing area in which different pastors at ICM will give different opinions. I've tried to describe the reality of a disciple at ICM. Practically, all disciples must lead at least one cell. For clarity sake, it's best to distinguish between a "disciple in process" (someone who might not be leading a cell at the present time) and "one of the 12" (one who is leading a cell).

[5] César Castellanos, *Sueña y Ganarás el Mundo*, 91-92.

[6] Luis Salas will not allow any of his potential disciples to graduate from the first semester of the School of Leadership unless he or she is leading a cell group. If they haven't "borne fruit" by that time, Salas often terminates the relationship.

[7] Luis Salas, cell seminar presented at the Republic Church, Quito, Ecuador, November 1998.

[8] César Castellanos, *Anointing for Multiplication*, audiotape.

[9] César Castellanos, *Successful Leadership through the G-12 Model*, audiotape.

[10] Ibid.

[11] César Castellanos, *The Cell Method through the Groups of Twelve*, audiotape.

[12] Pastor Castellanos ministers to his disciples every Monday (even though there are always more than 12 present). Following the example of their pastor, the 12 of César care for those under them and the care pattern continues throughout the church.

[13] César Castellanos, "Exploring the Groups of Twelve," 24.

[14] Luis Salas, cell seminar presented at the Republic Church, Quito, Ecuador, November 1998.

[15] Ibid.

[16] I have yet to discover a "discipleship material" that all G-12 groups use at ICM. It's the norm for each G-12 leader to use his own material according to the needs of the group. I witnessed the G-12 meeting of César Fajardo, which met after the morning worship service. I sensed obedience and interaction, but nothing like an in-depth, systematic approach to Bible. It's possible, however, to convert the G-12 system into a powerful discipleship structure. But in practice, the word *care* and *pastoring* better describes the G-12 system.

CHAPTER 5

[1] Luis Salas, cell seminar presented at the Republic Church, Quito, Ecuador, November 1998.

[2] César Castellanos, *Sueña y Ganarás el Mundo*, 101.

[3] Frank Gonzalez, *What is a Cell Group?* audiotape.

[4] Mercedes de Acevedo, *Developing Leaders in order to Develop Others*, audiotape of lecture presented at the Fourth Convention of Multiplication and Revival, January 1999.

[5] César Castellanos, *Sueña y Ganarás el Mundo*, p. 96.

[6] Ibid., 95.

[7] César Castellanos, "Exploring the Groups of Twelve," 24.

[8] César Fajardo and Lucho Salas, email to author, June 1998.

[9] César Castellanos, *Sueña y Ganarás el Mundo*, 95.

[10] Luis Salas, cell seminar presented at the Republic Church, Quito, Ecuador, November 1998.

[11] The church gives a very general invitation, almost to the point of even asking the newcomers to come forward, whether or not the person has received Christ. Why? Because in another room, trained workers diligently go through the plan of salvation. In other words, they don't expect the person in the large service to really know what he or she is doing. They simply cast the net in the general invitation and then draw it in during the consolidation time afterwards.

[12] If Mary were a young professional, she would take the same lessons from the young professional department.

[13] César Castellanos, "Exploring the Groups of Twelve," 24.

[14] Ibid.

[15] César Castellanos, *Sueña y Ganarás el Mundo* 104. José Maria Villanueva, *The Development of the Encounters*, audiotape.

[16] César Fajardo, *The Vision*, audiotape.

[17] José Maria Villanueva, *The Development of the Encounters*, audiotape.

[18] Claudia Castellanos, *Encounter Retreat: The Discipleship Base*, audiotape of lecture presented at the Fourth Convention of Multiplication and Revival, January 1999 and José Maria Villanueva, *The Development of the Encounters*, audiotape.

[19] César Castellanos, "Exploring the Groups of Twelve," 24.

[20] José Maria Villanueva, *The Development of the Encounters*, audiotape.

[21] Claudia Castellanos, *Encounter Retreat: The Discipleship Base*, audiotape.

[22] César Castellanos, *Sueña y Ganarás el Mundo*, 104.

[23] José Maria Villanueva, *The Development of the Encounters*, audiotape.

[24] César Fajardo mentioned to me that speaking in tongues is essential to cell leadership. César Castellanos says the same thing in *Sueña y Ganarás el Mundo*, 104, as well as Claudia Castellanos in *Encounter Retreat: The Discipleship Base*, audiotape.

[25] Claudia Castellanos, *Encounter Retreat: The Discipleship Base*, audiotape.

[26] Ibid.

[27] One year ago, ICM offered four lessons that dealt with how to deal with temptation, spiritual warfare, how to live a holy life (especially as it relates to dealing with non-Christian friends) and how to administer finances.

[28] Castellanos says that before teaching these Post-Encounter lessons, 70% of the people left the church in two to three months after attending an Encounter Retreat. Since the Post-Encounters, Pastor Castellanos says that they now conserve 100% of the fruit (César Castellanos, videotape of cell seminar presented in Quito, Ecuador, May 1998.). This percentage appears extremely high, nor can I be sure of its statistical validity. It is, however, an actual quote from César Castellanos.

[29] Mercedes de Acevedo, *Developing Leaders in order to Develop Others*, audiotape.

[30] Ibid. ICM uses often quotes Matthew Henry and Derek Prince in their teaching.

[31] Ibid.

[32] César Fajardo, *The Vision*, audiotape.

[33] Mercedes de Acevedo, *Developing Leaders in order to Develop Others*, audiotape.

[34] In October 1996, attendance at a second Encounter Retreat was only a requirement for the youth cells group leaders. By March 1997, the whole church required the second retreat. It is common knowledge at ICM that the ministry of the young people is the most effective in the entire church, and that an idea must first be proven among the young people before being implemented in the entire church.

[35] These "Theological Education by Extension" courses (called F.L.E.T.-Faculty of Latin American Theological Training) are developed by conservative Episcopalians in Argentina and are used throughout Latin America.

[36] They've stopped this teaching because they discovered that those taking higher leadership were not multiplying cell groups, nor were they learning about the vision of the church.

CHAPTER 6

[1] "Colombia," State Department Report, 1996. [internet site], [cited June 1999], www.travel.state.gov.

[2] During a meal in February 1997, César Castellanos told Ralph Neighbour, Jr. and myself that he desires to change the reputation of Colombia through the ministry of his church. During one of his presentation to Bethany World Prayer Center in June 1996, he asked those present to forgive him and Colombia for the awful atrocities committed there. César Fajardo once gave the illustration of how the Spanish conquerors planned on using Colombia as their strategic point to conquer the rest of Latin America. In the same way, Fajardo said, "We believe that God wants to use ICM to win the rest of the world through the cell strategy" (César Fajardo, *The Vision*, audiotape.).

[3] César Catellanos, videotape of cell seminar presented in Quito, Ecuador, May 1998.

[4] César Castellanos, *Transitioning to the Cell Church Philosophy*, audiotape.

[5] César Castellanos, *10 Commandments for Cell Group*, video.

[6] Claudia Castellanos, videotape of cell seminar presented in Quito, Ecuador, May 1998.

[7] Luis Salas, cell seminar presented at the Republic Church, Quito, Ecuador, November 1998.

[8] Mike Atkins, "G-12 Strategy Paper," e-mail to author, September 1998.

[9] There is no set time for a group to multiply at ICM, but according to my questionnaire, it takes an average of four to five months.

[10] Luis Salas said that they now give a questionnaire to the host of the cell to determine if the cell truly exists. It appears that some leaders were producing large numbers of cells that weren't functioning. In March 1999 that there were only 18,000 small groups, each with more than 6 people (Luis Salas, email to author, March 1999).

[11] Ibid.

[12] Many adults like Carlos occasionally attend the Saturday night youth service.

[13] I'm using the name "Javier" in this interview because he chose not to reveal his real name.

[14] Luis Salas, cell seminar presented at the Republic Church, Quito, Ecuador, November 1998.

[15] In part, Luis has chosen to maintain his full-time computer work. In March 1999 when I visited ICM, Luis told me that he had recently approached César Castellanos about

coming on staff full-time. Luis is also a musician who leads his own Christian contemporary music group that has produced several tapes. Not surprisingly, Luis only sleeps about five hours per night.

CHAPTER 7

[1] Luis Salas is one of the 12 of César Castellanos who multiplied his one cell to 600 cells in only a few years.

[2] Advanced Cell Training Three Seminar (Houston, TX: TOUCH Outreach Ministries, Inc., 1998), p. 14-15 of Day 1 Session 4.

[3] This one point is repeated over and over again from the top leadership at ICM — not just César Castellanos. I'm becoming more convinced that this is perhaps the key principle at ICM.

[4] For complete information on this topic, please read my book, *Home Cell Group Explosion: How Your Small Group Can Grow and Multiply* (TOUCH Outreach Ministries, Houston, TX, 1998). In a nutshell, I discovered that successful cell leaders, who multiplied their group, spent more time seeking God's face, dependent on Him for the direction of their cell group. They prepared themselves first and only afterwards, the lesson. They prayed diligently for their members, as well as non-Christian contacts. But successful cell leaders did not stop with prayer. They came down from the mountaintop to interact with real people, full of problems and pain. They pastored their cell members, visiting them regularly. They refused to allow the obstacles — that all cell leaders face — to overcome them. They fastened their eyes on one goal — reaching a lost world for Jesus through cell multiplication.

[5] Harold F. Weitsz, *Quest for the Perfect Pastoral System* (Little Falls, Roodepoort, South Africa: Little Falls Christian Centre, n.d.) 4.

[6] Ralph W. Neighbour Jr., "7 Barriers to Growth," *CellChurch*, Vol. 6, no. 3 (Summer 1997): 16.

[7] Advanced Cell Training Three Seminar.

[8] In the original cell model founded by David Cho, when five cells were formed, a supervisor was appointed to rotate among those five cells. The appointed supervisor was asked to stop leading his cell group in order to care for five groups. When five supervisors emerged (each over five cells), a zone pastor was appointed to care for those supervisors. This process of appointment continued upward to the office of district pastor who cared for the zone pastors. No one rose higher unless he or she received an invitation to assume the position.

[9] This average comes from the fact that cells meet weekly at the Republic Church, while the G-12 groups must meet once per month. This means that at the Republic Church, G-12 groups meet bimonthly (G-12 leader meets with his disciples once per month and the disciples of the G-12 leader meet once per month with their disciples).

[10] Castellanos talks about homogenous groups as one of the seven key principles of the G-12 model (*The Cell Method through the Groups of Twelve*, audiotape).

[11] José Maria Villanueva, *The Development of the Encounters*, audiotape.

CHAPTER 8

[1] James M. Kourzes & Barry Z. Posner, *The Leadership Challenge: How to Keep Getting Extraordinary Things Done in Organizations* (San Francisco, CA: Jossey-Bass Publishers, 1995), 9-10.

[2] Not every church bases cell lessons on the Sunday morning sermon. Karen Hurston points out that Yoido Full Gospel Church originally used Cho's expository messages from the Wednesday evening meetings. Later key leaders prepared the cell lessons based on Cho's teaching in general. The majority of cell churches worldwide, however, use the Sunday morning message as the basis for the weekly cell lesson.

[3] Understand that this is the ideal. I've observed that the 5x5 numbering is not always observed. Elim, for example, had eight zone pastors (instead of five) under each district pastor.

[4] Distinctions between the 5x5 and G-12 models:

FOUNDATIONAL PRINCIPLES	5x5 Structure	G-12 Structure
LEADERSHIP TRAINING	Potential leaders are trained within the cell and through seminars before beginning cell leadership. Ongoing (often weekly) training takes in the zones and districts.	Potential leaders are trained through Encounter Retreats and School of Leadership (see chapter five).
GEOGRAPHICAL DIVISION	Cell groups are divided into geographical areas under district pastors, zone leaders, and section supervisors.	Cell groups are divided in homogeneous groups: men, women, couples, young professionals, youth, adolescents, and children. The G-12 system flows down from each homogeneous category.
JETHRO SYSTEM	Top leadership is raised up to pastor cell leaders under them. The names of these leaders are: district pastors, zone pastors, supervisors (or section leaders) and cell leaders.	There are only two titles: G-12 leader and cell leader. Very successful G-12 leaders (as measured in cell multiplication) are invited to serve on the pastoral staff.
MULTIPLICATION	Certain gifted members are appointed as future leaders and guide the newly formed daughter cell. Mother-daughter cell multiplication is the norm. The cell gives birth to another cell when the parent cell reaches a certain size.	Every member is expected to eventually lead a cell group. When the person finishes training he or she starts a cell group. Size of the parent cell is not an issue.
CENTRAL PLANNING	Cell group planning takes place on a centralized level in district offices.	Cell group planning is primarily handled through each G-12 group under the different homogeneous departments.
CELL LEADER CARE	Cell Leaders are cared for by district pastors, zone pastors, and supervisors.	Leaders are cared for by leaders of twelve from the lower levels all the way up to the twelve disciples of Pastor Castellanos.

The 5x5 model focuses on the size of a group and giving birth to daughter cells — exact replicas of the parent cells. In the 5x5 model, the parent group prepares to give birth to a daughter cell. Assistant leaders are chosen and trained to lead daughter cell groups. The following table highlights the strengths and weaknesses of the two models.

Strengths and weaknesses of the two models:

5x5 Model	G-12 Model
STRENGTHS	
• Better chance of cell survival • Good control & easier management • Simple structure to understand (Clear) • Good Pastoral (care) structure and communication • Not time taxing • Promotion path is clear • Territorial, focused & defined planned leadership promotion	• Evangelism focused • Weekly Leadership meetings (more personal contact) • Emphasis on new leadership • Cell planting concept • Faster growth potential • Focus on homogenous groups • Non-geographical
WEAKNESSES	
• Weak members can hide forever • Working relationships severed at multiplication • Geographical boundary emphasis • Multiple levels create distance between pastors, cell leaders and members • Need more full time Pastors • Slower leadership development • Some homogenous groups are overlooked	• Quality of leadership could diminish • Quality of meetings could diminish • Monitoring/Care process weakens • Enforced relationships (sometimes unwanted fixed relationships) • Time pressures • A sense of loss of control • Potentially weak Cells
OPPORTUNITIES	
• Stable Church structure • Clear Ministry opportunities • Evangelism (Target groups)	• Rapid church growth • Cell planting (Homogenous) • Leadership development • Evangelism (Target groups)

[5] The 5x5 structure normally adds paid staff at higher levels. However, as the system grows, more staff is added. This is not necessarily true, however. Love Alive Church *(Amor Viviente)* in Tegucigalpa, Honduras doesn't even pay their district pastors. All cell positions are voluntary, except for the role of "cell director" (as of 1996-97).

[6] Larry Stockstill, *G-12 System,* audiotape of message presented at the National Cell Church Pastor's Conference, November 1998.

[7] Ralph Neighbour, Jr. "Structuring Your Church for Growth," *CellChurch,* Vol. 7, no. 2 (Spring 1998): 15.

[8] Mike Atkins.

[9] ICM, for example, reported incredible cell growth in 1998 (24,000) and later had to change the statistics to adjust to reality in the beginning of 1999 (20,000).

[10] The shepherding movement of the 1970s taught obedience to leadership. In this movement a "disciple" had to obey the leader and submit to his or her direction. Individual freedom and initiative were not highly esteemed, and many leaders controlled their disciples.

CHAPTER 9

[1] "Oneworld," [internet site], [cited 6 April 1999], www.oneworld.org.

[2] César Castellanos, *Sueña y Ganarás el Mundo*, 87.

[3] Ibid., 86.

[4] Ralph W. Neighbour Jr. email to author, 27 November 1998. I agree with Neighbour. Some mistakenly see the G-12 structure as functioning apart from the cell system. If your G-12 system functions apart from the pastoral care of your cell system, you're creating two separate systems and opening the door for all kinds of confusion. Some people think that you can disciple people in the G-12 model that are different from your cell leaders. But who would these disciples be? You'd soon have conflict.

[5] *The New Bible Dictionary* (Wheaton, Illinois: Tyndale House Publishers, Inc.), 1962, s.v. "disciple."

[6] Actually, ICM teaches that you make your disciples into your image (César Castellanos, *Successful Leadership through the G-12 Model*, audiotape). Yes, ICM will probably clarify this by saying that you your disciples to be like you because you are like Christ, which is biblical. Yet, caution is in order here.

[7] César Castellanos, *Successful Leadership through the G-12 Model*, audiotape.

[8] One pastor in a G-12 church questioned the whole idea of calling 12 people your disciples who you have not personally led to the Lord. He felt it was strange that one could go around picking their disciples when these same people had been discipled by many other people. This particular pastor felt that a disciple was someone that you won to Christ and had trained to become a cell leader. He felt that the goal of a church should be for every member to make one such disciple per year.

[9] César Castellanos and the pastors at ICM will tell you that the vision of the number 12 came directly from God, and therefore you must follow it. They often justify this particular number by referring to a direct revelation from God.

[10] Larry Stockstill, *The Principle of the 12*, audiotape of message presented at the National Cell Church Pastor's Conference, November 1997.

[11] Jay Firebaugh, e-mail to author, 9 April 1999.

CHAPTER 10

[1] Jeannette Buller, "Cell Church" [internet site], [cited June 1999], www.cell-church.org.

[2] I believe that you can even apply the G-12 principles in your church without drastically changing your cell church structure. If you are using the 5x5 structure, you can simply adapt that structure by using G-12 principles. You might call it the G-5 model.

[3] All of the statistics for the 12 churches in chapters 10-11 reflect their growth as of the first quarter of 1999.

[4] Tim Scheuer, e-mail to author, 28 April 1999.

[5] Ibid.

[6] Advanced Cell Training Four Seminar (Houston, TX: TOUCH Outreach Ministries, Inc, 1998), p. 14-15 of Day 1, Session 4.

[7] Brad Shedd, email to author, June 1999.

[8] Pastor Larry's book, *The Cell Church* (Ventura, CA: Regal Books, 1998) dedicates one entire chapter to the G-12 model. In my book *Reap the Harvest* (Houston, TX: TOUCH Publications, 1999) I talk about BWPC's transition to the G-12 model in the appendix.

Home Cell Group Explosion (Houston, TX: TOUCH Publications, 1998) also deals with the G-12 model at BWPC.

9 We must remember that the early growth and excitement at Bethany didn't come as much from the G-12 model as the new emphasis on homogeneous cells. The vast majority of the over 500 new groups that BWPC has started since transitioning to the G-12 model are homogeneous groups. These groups are based around special interests such as sports, work, or school. Homogenous groups are an effective way to evangelize and disciple non-Christians. Most Americans know people at work, not their neighbors. BWPC still maintains their geographical distinction, while having the liberty to start homogenous groups.

10 Billy Hornsby, *Activity: Maintenance-Growth*, audiotape of lecture presented in the "Holding the Harvest Series," January 1998.

11 "Leadership Summit," Bethany World Prayer Center, August 1999.

12 Billy Hornsby, email to author, 24 November 1998

13 Larry Stockstill, *G-12 System*, audiotape.

CHAPTER 11

1 Kouzes and Posner, *The Leadership Challenge*, xviii.

2 Personally, I believe that the equipping track of Little Falls Christian Centre is one of best equipping tracks on the cell church market today. Every potential leader can attend the training track consisting of four weekend encounters spread over a four-month period. The weekend encounters repeat continuously throughout the year and enables each member to select four weekends suitable to his or her lifestyle and other commitments. One can therefore complete the four encounters in a four month period or longer.

Preceding each encounter weekend, each member receives a process booklet with questions to answer. After completion of this booklet, the cell leader reviews it and signs it, thus permitting the member to attend the encounter weekend. Thus, the booklet becomes the "entry ticket" for the appropriate encounter weekend and qualifies the person to receive the weekend training manual.

The four encounter weekends cover basic concepts of Christianity, spiritual freedom and victory, soul winning and cell leadership training. Each weekend is held in the church, starts on Friday night, and finishes on Saturday. The member must faithfully attend his cell meeting to fulfill the assignments of the weekend. Once the course has been completed the new leader is expected to attend the quarterly general leadership training weekend.

After becoming a cell leader, further training takes place for zone supervisors, and the two-year course of the LFCC College for Advanced Christian Education must be completed by all who emerge as new potential pastors from the ranks of the Zone Supervisors. Newly trained potential leaders may begin their own cells, connecting them to the current Jethro type structure or are even encouraged to plant new cells at the workplace, or places of sport and other interests. Many become intern cell leaders and are able to take new cells immediately after completing the training track. The equipping track is capable of training hundreds of new cell leaders per year.

The largest missions and evangelism organization in South Africa, Jesus Alive Ministries, under the leadership of Evangelist Peter Pretorius, is now translating the entire LFCC equipping track into several African languages on DVD, with 2,000 DVD players and screens to be placed at 2,000 training points for leaders in Africa. This will ultimately be increased to 7,000 training points. This project will promote G-12 church planting and development in Africa. Jesus Alive Ministries has already seen more than 4,000,000 souls won for Christ in Africa, and will now endeavor to place the thousands of converts in the hands of G-12 trained leaders all over the continent.

[3] Neville Chamberlain, ed., *Cell Church Missions Network News Roundup #43*, e-mail to author, June 1999.

[4] According to Abbalove, the former vertical structure caused stagnation and decline of the church, usually after five to seven years according to Eddy's previous experience. For example, if one leader somewhere down the chain decides to make trouble, he could lead all those under him away. This is why this model always requires a very strong leader at the top to keep everyone in line. Abbalove found that if a leader moved to another city, it was not easy to fill the gap in the chain. Furthermore, in the previous G-12-like model a person could effectively learn from only one person (his immediate leader) all his life, which is not a healthy, balanced pattern.

[5] Jerry Smith, email to Ralph Neighbour, 26 February 1998.

[6] Others on staff felt that they should let go of the geographical divisions and concentrate solely on ministries, so as to allow the G-12 model to naturally flow from these new divisions.

[7] At CCG, it takes approximately six month (two trimesters) to lead a cell group.

CHAPTER 12

[1] Jim Egli, "What Do I Do with the G-12 Model?" *CellChurch*. Vol. 7, no. 4 (Fall 1998): 26-27.

[2] Jerry Smith, email to Ralph Neighbour, 26 February 1998.

[3] Most people using Encounter Retreats are not following the precise three-day retreat pattern of ICM.

[4] This science relates to how changes are diffused into a particular culture or organization, best captured in Everett M. Rogers, *Diffusion of Innovations*, 4th Ed. (New York: The Free Press, 1995).

[5] Jim Egli, "What Do I Do with the G-12 Model?" 26-27.

[6] Ibid.

[7] Ibid.

APPENDIX A

[1] César Castellanos, *Sueña y Ganarás el Mundo*, 177.

[2] Luis Salas, interview by author, 28 November 1998.

[3] Ibid.

[4] Randall Neighbour, email to author, 14 April 1998.

[5] Mike Atkins.

[6] Alan Creech, "Cell Church" [internet site], [cited December 1998], www.cell-church.org.

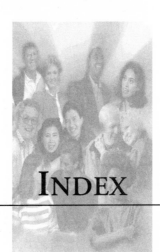

INDEX

Special Savings!

Additional Cell Resources by Joel Cosmiskey available from TOUCH Publications